Anniversary Snow

楊煉　　　Yang Lian

Anniversary Snow

周年之雪

translated from Chinese by Brian Holton

and

W.N. Herbert, L. Leigh, Liang Lizhen, Pascale Petit,
Fiona Sampson, George Szirtes, Joshua Weiner

Shearsman Books

First published in the United Kingdom in 2019 by
Shearsman Books
50 Westons Hill Drive
Emersons Green
BRISTOL
BS16 7DF

Shearsman Books Ltd Registered Office
30–31 St. James Place, Mangotsfield, Bristol BS16 9JB
(this address not for correspondence)

www.shearsman.com

ISBN 978-1-84861-670-7

Poems copyright © Yang Lian, 2019
Translations copyright © Brian Holton, 2019
Further translations copyright © W.N. Herbert, L. Leigh, Liang Lizhen,
Pascale Petit, Fiona Sampson, George Szirtes and Joshua Weiner, 2019

The right of Yang Lian to be identified as the author of this volume, and of Brian Holton, W.N. Herbert, L. Leigh, Liang Lizhen, Pascale Petit, Fiona Sampson, George Szirtes and Joshua Weiner to be identified as the translators thereof, has been asserted by them in accordance with the Copyrights, Designs and Patents Act of 1988.
All rights reserved.

Translator's Acknowledgements
Brian Holton would like to thank the Emily Harvey Foundation for their generous offer of a Venice Residency, during which this book was finished. Thanks must also go to Yang Lian, as always, for his unfailing willingness to help make these translations better. We have been working together for a quarter of a century now, and it has been a great adventure for both of us.

CONTENTS

SHORT POEMS

Ocarina: To the Listener in the Dark	11
A Line on the Liangzhu Jade Cong	13
Questions About the Demon Taotie	15
Wicked King Zhou of Shang's Sacrificial Dog Pit	17
Homage to Du Fu's Cottage	19
Grandmother's Boat	21
Yongle Plum Blossom Vase	24
Night on Gongchen Bridge	26
Jin Sha	28

⊕

A Sunflower Seed's Lines of Negation	29
Three Political Poems	
1. Baby Girl	30
2. Blood and Coal	31
3. Meditation	32
Kaifeng / Open Sealed	
1. Kai / Open	33
2. Feng / Sealed	34
3. Kai / Open	35
4. Feng / Sealed	36
Tranquil Studio: A Contemporary Piece for Guqin	37
Yellow Mountain Freeze-Frame	39
Shanshui Legend	40
The Train East	42
Imperial Garden Hungry Ghost Festival	44

South Gate Hungry Ghost Festival	45
The Hills That Grew Up With Me	46
Dialect Writing	48
Dialeck Scrievin – Anither Wey	49

⊕

Butterfly—Nabokov	51
Butterfly—Berlin	53
Butterfly—Old Age	55
Bird: Research into Origins	57
Dance: Swimming Naked with Li Bai	59
St. Andrews	62
U1, Station *New Songs From a Jade Terrace*	64
Words on a Potsherd in the Platonic Academy	66
The Cry of Cranes in Bassdorf	68
Butterfly Lake	70
Guarding the Moon	71
I Know a Handful of Earth	72
Four Glacier Poems	
1. Glacier Poem: Moonstone	73
2. Glacier Poem: Black Tongue Jottings	74
3. Glacier Poem: Downhill	75
4. Glacier Poem: Spirituals	76
Moscow: An Almost Ballad	78
Peter the Great's Seagull	81
River Rhine – A "Blue Sky" Poem	83
Fado – The Sea's Return	85
Ocarina: Dark of the Listener	87
At Tranströmer's Grave	89

⊕

Parallel Astronomy	90
Sparkle Sonnet	92
Anniversary Snow	94
The Girl in the Museum	
1. In the Time of Carved Stone	96
2. One Arrow Flies Alone	97
3. Vase	98
4. Phidias's Horse Head	99
5. Girl Ghosting	100
6. The Great Moving Marble Screen	101
7. Birthday	102
8. The Dictionary Decodes Life	103
9. Beasts Standing And Walking	104
10. Group Photo	105
Swansea: Long View of the Blue at My Side	106
Deeply Embedded Little Epic	108
The Voice of Rain in Verona	110
Reed Letter	112

POEM SEQUENCES

You Don't Know the Colour of Snow (200 lines)	
1. You Don't Know (100 lines)	115
2. The Colour of Snow (100 lines)	119
Dirge	122
Flying Cornices of the Four-Bridge Misty Rain Pavilion	
1. Theme of Landscape	128
2. Theme of Time	129
3. Theme of Space	129
4. Theme of Solitude	130
5. In the Rain: Garden Where Paths Never Cross	131

Advanced Study
    1, A Moment of Licking   134
    2, Walk Through: Books of Bronze and Glass   135
    3, Poetic Inquiry – Another Embedded Voice   136
    4, Advanced Studies   137

Painting: Elegy with Spanning Bridge   139

Venice Elegy   144
    1. Fugitive Poem   145
    2. Rot Poem   146
    3. Graveyard Poem   147
    4. Sinking Poem   148
    5. Reflection: Tintoretto's Mirror   149

Translator's Afterword   152

短诗
SHORT POEMS

埙：致黑暗中的听者

OCARINA: TO THE LISTENER IN THE DARK[1]

there is no beginning   the stage is a prehistoric
retreat into imagination   retreating again to kissing
red-hot lips   stopping a mouth of clay   six millennia
a long line of verse rubs lovesick lungs   silken gleam
sparkles and jerks back the wild goose cry in your bosom   rehearsing
the ocarina's one and only night   faraway ghosts softly sing
        in the dark you sit   deep as the wilderness
        hear a fresh tenderness with nowhere to fall back

from one sound to the next the drawn-out dialect of ghosts
has erased so many people   rubbing   water's motion
surrounding   shielding the starry sky with the loneliness of water
an ocarina fills with a fleshly glow from beneath the grave
coldly blowing   you seep into the female purity of your own shade
darkly loving   every elegy a love song
        in the dark clouds stir as the little finger lifts
        you whisper like wreckage   vomit comfort

oh listen   the one and only story fired and formed in a kiln
sobs as it rehearses   that distant beauty on your body
a hole gives you back a single soaking
a tiny Saturn revolves   rings shattering
tonight   hearing's lines of force keep secrets
need we speak of weal or woe   as the score's yearned-for farewell kiss
        in darkness   the rare flowers of the dark are thriving
        floating   a single second dazzles with threats

the poetic   commands the listener to be like a singer   commands your breathing
being born   dying   the gift of clay

handed through time   you are here   spring breezes in your heart
mouth on mouth lovemaking sips the green that dyes the wilderness

and what's colourless   caresses grass tips   commands silence
overflows with echoes   those ripples   have no ending
    in the dark the melody yearns inch by inch for love
      carves   the one and only you   the one and only sound that's lingering

---

[1] *Translator's note*: The *xun*, which dates back to the Stone Age, is an egg-shaped wind instrument made of clay or bone, similar to an ocarina, but without the fipple mouthpiece. Yang Lian has been attempting to master this challenging instrument for some years.

一条良渚玉琮上的线

A LINE ON THE LIANGZHU JADE CONG

Translated by George Szirtes and Yang Lian

Jade wants to disappear – the carved world in its grip.
Lake-green skin wants to disappear – a strip

Of distant brilliance across the eye –
The line that depicts home also wipes it away

Straight – birds like shark's teeth graze the blue sky –
a precise tender body, so birds and hours fly

you're stitching space – time's needle-tip –
jade dust falls, noise of tsunami, the rip

of pain, of needle – dust falling grit by grit –
a tight network, the skull's shallow dip –

hard carving steeped in softness, *sulci* and *gyri*
hand enters shape, the teardrop's fragrance, now salty

now crispy – beads' brilliance to hold the circle's eye –
exposed target – five thousand years crystallised in a day.

returning only once, you're always about to quit –
like the burnished beauty of the knife's blood slit

with the light in the jade that leaks and silts up –
stone curtains drawn on centuries, time through a gap,

jade at its core is a face – desiring infinity
but infinity has died, as it must always die –

brute natural coral   whiteness   flooding brow-high-
home – the fixed idea, increasing intensity

staring as the tsunami rises in one huge fit –
the first character: one line paints it.

饕餮之问

QUESTIONS ABOUT THE DEMON TAOTIE[2]

Translated by Pascale Petit [3]

the Pole Star is set in the centre of his forehead.
the deep blue   is crystalline   his ice pupil
has destroyed everything   does the lonely
boiled girl embrace everything?

escaping from Anyang   is an escape into the Yin night
no other light except this sight
luxuriously grinding a huge axe
where did the tender broken limbs fall?

looking up   for thousands of years
we sink down   water always grinds its teeth
beneath us   the girl collapsing to a gurgle
does Taotie seize   or chew?

thousands of words re-split open are still
the one character   that one stroke captures life's flow
has been cooked ten thousand times   the flesh still soaked in sorrow
to reawaken   Is seizing   chewing?

this face is even more ruthless
than non-being   this powerlessness
staring out rams a hole
to pound away   What beauty is not bloody?

our floating life is carved
on the shallow bronze relief   Does

the pupil's axle icily shrink space?
how many suns don't rise or set in the darkness of naming?

the girl swings gracefully back from the Yin
night   does a thin fragrance snuff out all light?
do bestial and human faces gently clasp vapour?
has unutterable language   finally fulfilled the sacrifice?

---

[2] *Author's note*: This powerful, terrified face stares silently at you. It's made of bronze, the form is symmetrical, the look part human and part animal, but clearly with a supernatural power. It is *Taotie*, the most mysterious, odd but extremely exquisite design carved everywhere on bronzes made in the Shang Dynasty (16th–11th century BCE). But, are these designs just decorations? Then, why do they watch us from all possible angles like God(s)? Looking back at them, one can feel her/his present is sucked in and swallowed by the timeless ancient. In Anyang of Henan province, the site of Yin, the capital of the late Shang dynasty (after 13th century BCE), archaeologists found there were huge numbers of human sacrifices, at the same time as when the Chinese character-system suddenly began without any evidence of so-called prior "evolution". This ancient language has been used throughout the centuries and is still in use. When I arrived in Anyang that night, I couldn't help but jump into a taxi to run into the darkness of Yin, and feel that the Shang moon was still hanging above me. The poem is made up of questions and is about these questions; perhaps they are all we are so far.

[3] *Translator's note*: I translated this poem after descending into the subterranean vault of the Shanghai Museum with Yang Lian. The curator of bronzes brought in a large Shang dynasty taotie cauldron. As it was slowly unwrapped, we saw that there was a demon carved in low relief on the front and back of the vessel. He had tripod legs and verdigris cloud motifs around and inside his face. These cauldrons were thought to have been used for cannibalistic rites, but no one knew for sure if taotie was a god who demanded human sacrifice, since other finds in the old capital of Yin (now known as Anyang) reveal an advanced civilisation with the rudiments of early Chinese characters. I have a special interest in prehistoric artefacts and in demons, so this poem was a delight to work on and try to render in English. I do not speak Mandarin so the translation was done by talking through each line with Lian.

纣王的腰坑

WICKED KING ZHOU OF SHANG'S SACRIFICIAL DOG PIT

menstrual blood pooled under Daji[4]　　three thousand years crimson
crimson for three thousand more　　until it equals Daji's glance
come　　pour wine　　on the jade bowl that observes us dark crane wings flap
oh how fine the snowy wrist that started the fire　　the butterfly-embroidered gown

　　　　a funnel quietly dripping
　　　　the Stag Stage treasure house upended[5]

words made redundant　　as the human shape is redundant
sitting hugging jewellery　　gold and silver　　worse to sit hugging a fireball
from the pagoda's ascending pinnacle to its descending pinnacle　　a slim
waist　　pillowed on height　　gyring oh　　whose limbs dance our land

　　　　a funnel quietly dripping
　　　　a beauty politely repudiated

treading tongues of flame the tomb passage descends　　the pit's depth
only a little deeper than death　　black as the yellow earth's sighing
repeating　　no need for a guide dog　　the king sacrificed himself pulling
the probe of white bone downward　　countenance cold-water ice

　　　　a funnel quietly dripping
　　　　a world vomited up

now lovely cheeks have caught fire too　　like a wild longing for a lover
now words so close at hand move bright coloured shades
Daji's poem inhales lovers' hurried and eager odes
a backward glance　　a glimpse of a life brimming over

17

    a funnel quietly dripping
    all   heaven and earth look on each other and smile

11 November 2010

[4.] *Translator's note*: Daji, also known as Fu Hao, Lady Hao, or, posthumously, Mu Xin (died c.1200 BCE), was one of the many wives of King Wu Ding of the Shang dynasty: she served as an army general and high priestess.

[5] *Translator's note*: The pavilion complex Lu Tai, also known as Deer Terrace, was set alight in 1046 BCE by King Zhou: the Shang dynasty ended with his death in the flames: he was consumed along with all his treasures.

谒草堂

HOMAGE TO DU FU'S COTTAGE[6]

Translated by L. Leigh, revised by Brian Holton

1
thirty years   walking from this side of summer to the other side
thirty years   fermenting autumn colours

a glass of stronger wine
set before me   reflects a swallowed smile

gardenia fragrance still sews up cracked dusk
the cottage like a straw boat   listening   to the sound of waters of my own

running past   but never out of
a deep shady green pond's sighing diameter

my strolling breath caresses low bamboo leaves
as I count the scattered raindrops   falling neatly into death

thirty years ago the child   turned away leaving the whirlpool
the flowery path once again   the wooden door once again

board the boats of poets' own distinct deaths
painfully scrape here this river bed thirteen hundred years old

light as a blade of grass   despite what the wild wind carved
he didn't reject the tragic endgame poverty and illness

presented to him   the millstone he pushed
grinds chimney smoke

that faintly floats and diffuses   my maturity
is like a nation   grown accustomed to the beauty of sorrow

2
a line of poetry's dim corridor goes darker and darker
a line of poetry   in the quiet garden tourists have dispersed
the grove's bamboo stems touch the sound of wind   of rain   of birds
drenched wild flowers like drenched human forms
give me a gloaming   seeping through yellowing paper
that waited thirty years   seeping through two faces pushed further apart
by two waters   a wooden bed a cold quilt
catch up with the swallows   a faintly scented space endlessly bows out
into meaning lit up in leaked-away flesh and blood
give me a life   unlike any other path
but change all paths to shadow   he walks slowly
throws beside me raindrops big as wine glasses
clouds darken   one candle's light shines up from the water's depths
one summer's chill plays back a thousand summers
give me the strength   to forget poetry and only then return to
the sweet warmth that pierces bone   a death more startling than language
corrupted by worthless living now become hollow words
yet the sea's edge I have carefully trodden presses closely on
his spare silhouette   forgetting to pay homage to a thatched cottage
thirty years before trivially putting up a bit of a thatched cottage
an endless line of poetry has used up the word vagrant
a history   without scenes of ruin and desolation
as the lamps of a thousand homes sacrifice in the heart of a night so deep
and nip buds tender and wet   forming in the same instant
give me bright scarlet   a fragrance kept within
exuding this moment   stars flicker and germinate
I am already that old and beautiful pure and clean enough person

---

[6] *Translator's note*: This refers to the cottage in Chengdu, Sichuan, where the great poet Du Fu lived, CE760-CE764.

奶奶的船

GRANDMOTHER'S BOAT[7]

Translated by Yang Lian with Lizhen Liang and Fiona Sampson

A tune from Guangling[8] and the soaking waists of the palace maids towing the boats.
The glamour of waterside willows sinking into the Grand Canal.
The tiny reincarnated womb   approaches once more.
Mild internal injuries by small footprints   on this flight of bluestone stairs
bound curves embroidered   under hulls   in another century
the cry of a startled crane is knocked up deep into the night.

That crane of yours   floated   above the year 1897.
The Lord and the little lady arrived with the stream   anchored for a night
answering the bright moon and a vision of splendour   anchored for two nights
the peaks of Shugang Ridge[9] gleam through green hills stretched out through your
          life anchored for three nights   you waited for me in a lotus seed,
onstage at three.   Applying and removing its makeup   the river
was spreading a painted scroll.

Destination of your future   and of your past   the boat's masts
pointed to the Pole Star   the waters of Dongting Lake   the waters of the Yuan
                    and Li Rivers,
overtaking the lightning-flash of that flowery snake   in the small dark room with no
                                        window.
No fire accompanied your last breath   an old servant's tears
wiped away without your noticing in the dusk   between the fragrant carved
                              camphorwood partitions.
Bleakness signalled from the underworld   distance froze the bone marrow.

From a duplicate water-mark I identify
your naivety at anchor   still smiling.   That Mongolian light in your eyes.

Father   holding me   and the poem of your absence in this one line
gone over by heart once again   in the accent of a handful of tuberose,
building up while tearing down the intrinsic tenderness of a little girl
that casts the finest shadow onto those sculling women.

Stepping through Dongquan Gate[10]   a long alley crowded with farewells.
Stepping in from the House of Rockeries[11]   the moon overlooking the water
waxing full whenever it wants   letting the drowned poets stroll underwater.
Stepping in from the word Yangzhou   full of the smell of salt
through the carved window lattice   through the rails   Grandmother's boat
                                    moored at the dock.
Listen   to never-ending three years old.   The wild waves

Crush   and long-ago crushed the breathing recorded by the stone steps.
My breath   comes looking for you, unreachable in your rare flowering.
Leaning close to you for once   for me you emerge   on your sickbed
fate gathered in your yellowish-white palms.   The world's water
leaks into this one drop   Granny.   The stinging warmth
remains   when the wake of your small body has flattened out.

I'm already on board.   Sweet fishy blood and bone.
A word is settled   a fluid glance lingers in the snow and wind
the revenant's faint sigh is contained for thousands of miles
a glistening epitaph returns wherever access is granted.
You remain in such serenity,   Granny.   No matter how far away I heave out
                                    the sails
you sail ahead   navigating with your crane wing-tips.

[7] *Author's note*: My grandmother was in Yangzhou when she was three years old, and I imagined she was brought by boat from Beijing to here, stopped a while, then continued on to south China. However young she was, my father, myself (my poems) and 20th century Chinese history were all inside her (womb), together with her own sad life later. This poem is a small but epic piece of Chinese history.

[8] *Author's note*: A surviving Guqin melody most commonly attributed to the famous essayist and poet Xi Kang (CE223–262). It had its source in another title called 'Nie Zheng Stabs the Han King to Avenge the Murder of His Father'. The *guqin* (pronounced goo-chin) is a horizontal harp, the favourite instrument of the literati. *Guangling* is the ancient name of Yangzhou, on record from the Han Dynasty (BCE202–CE220).

[9] *Author's note*: The three peaks of Shugang Ridge traverse the northern suburbs of Yangzhou. The peaks, covered by millions of green pines and verdant cypresses, have as their centrepiece the Daming Temple, dotted with halls, terraces and towers as well as waterside pavilions.

[10] *Author's note*: A quiet ancient back alley in Yangzhou that contains a host of sites, the main gate of which dates back to the Qing Dynasty (1644–1911). It thankfully lacks any sense of commercialization though small restaurants and craft shops line the alley.

[11] *Author's note*: The only existing example of a structure built by the great 17th century master painter Shi Tao, it is a marvellously creative artificial rockery excelling nature. There is a man-made moon reflected on the pool beside the stone house, which is a super-secluded place to hide away from the summer heat.

永乐梅瓶

YONGLE PLUM BLOSSOM VASE[12]

Translated by L. Leigh, revised by Brian Holton

an invisible plum blossom branch stops here to wait for me
two loving hands   built up the texture of jade   to caress
then I changed   six hundred early winters piled up the first snows
seeping blue a shivering night   a vase's slim waist warmly
nestles into the world's edge   I am startled awake in my billowing clouds
a beauty's shoulder probes into roaring flames probes into blood-red
invisible dragon claws press down deadly hard   this downfall

a beauty from passion born   a trace of red floods her cheeks
from plum   from fire   one night in a dragon kiln
dragon eyes   embedded in my naked body   look down at life
carve in secrecy a desire to be toyed with   petals
beastlike little claw points tiptoe on crystal branches
beauty   empties us out   search   burn
endure   the pain that forces a vase to dazzle the eye

             so my deep contemplation is also invisible to others
I stand upright   holding my breath   a sylphlike poem
embroiders dynasties   voices   on my body
endless reflected paths of beacon fires slide off like praise
does it concern me?   those misprints cataclysmic change or rise and fall
are all deleted into my body   a deeply inhaled circle
inhaling the world   oh come   shatter into my scarlet

a museum surrounds this bud   faint aroma floats and drifts
oh   soak up sorrow   the beauty's flesh and skin
takes form each night   a whiff of aroma licks through dragon's moans   tsunami
strips me sculpts me   a plum dance lingers on an extreme
wait another six hundred years   love still fresh and tender   at one stroke
uses up the passing ages   bloody fingerprints flutter   twist and turn   steady
an invisible branch of plum blossom is coruscatingly implanted everywhere

[12] *Translator's note*: The title refers to the one and only Ming dynasty Yongle period (1402–1424) copper-red dragon plum vase (Mei Ping) which was exhibited in the British Museum in 2016. The literal translation of *Yongle* is "forever happiness".

拱宸桥一夜

NIGHT ON GONGCHEN BRIDGE[13]

how many beauties there are at West Lake
then how much darkness will overflow from the Grand Canal's body
picking clean this abrupt silver white collarbone

Shuyu Café's sycamore tongue tips
write in the dark   we lean on a stone balustrade
a stone balustrade leans on a world   drifting   yet bottomless

Gongchen Bridge   the fan I open in the sky
flapped once   a millennium-old rice wine blots out ink-black
flapped twice   water's wires draw the galaxy back

sighing's light speed hidden before   behind
who then?   tearful locked-up eyes sip locked-up longing
in the poem's name an eyeful of looking far

a drop   brims over to drown a city's dozing
standing one time proud and high   a fragrant garden facing its jail time
a Southland heading for the North

how many tender caresses there are too in so much shame
who bowed heads on the bridge   then heard outpouring night and day
oh, nothing to be done   tonight   dark as Solitary Hill

is someone climbing up? Gongchen Bridge fleets past loaded with the starry sky
we're wrapped in the ghostly chill
fallen in love with an impossible glimmering

a collarbone gently sucks unstoppable pain
grows   West Lake's shoulders   wings   plumage
the blackest aesthetic is the most boundless

[13] *Translator's note*: Gongchen Bridge spans the Grand Canal. Built in 1631, it is the tallest and highest of the ancient bridges in the city of Hangzhou. Its name means *Rising to Guard the Stars*.

金沙

JIN SHA[14]

they are all dead   yet the dark shadows of the huge trees live on
as animals   the distant past   brims over the railings like a valley
swallows down your imagination   lung-chillingly imagining
tonight   another world of salty stench and fishy stink

death flattens the dead   hidden-away eyes
stare deeper and snuggle into our bosom
golden masks every second   bequeath   squash
muttering   one star in the deep black sky

like a word long ago taken away   can look back at your
shivering   all over your body   this light mist
sips in the mouth of a grain of sand   cry out if you like
a ghostly aesthetic   not saying has a light-speed of unsayability

driving here painfully slowly   the tiny car park
infinitely large   a pair of outer space bird's cogwheel-set hearts
brake a precision-carved night of departed souls
crystal night   again and again cats' ears swivel to the distance

here is furthest away   the purest of deaths
rotates   breaths crashed into units of millennia
have learned to cherish reconstructed colourlessness   cock crow
arranges for us to lie down in a seabed where the sea is invisible

---

[14] *Translator's note*: Archaeological site in Chengdu, Sichuan. The Jinsha culture flourished around BCE 1000.

一粒葵花籽的否定句

A SUNFLOWER SEED'S LINES OF NEGATION

For Ai Weiwei

unimaginable that Du Fu's little boat was once
moored on this ceramic river
I don't know the moonlight   see only the poem's clarity
attenuated line by line   to a non-person
to the symbols   discussing and avoiding everything
I'm no symbol   a sun dying under the sunflower seed's hard shell
nor is the sun   snow-white collapsed meat of children
nor have I disappeared   daybreak's horizon impossibly
forgot that pain   bones like glass sliced by glass
I didn't scream, so must scream at each first light
an earthquake never stands still
no need to suffocate the dead   planting rows of fences to the ends of the earth
handcuffing ever more shameful silence   so   I don't fear
the young policewoman interrogating my naked body
it was formed by fire   no different to yours
knowing no other way to shatter but a hundred million shatterings within myself
falling into no soil   only into the river that can't flow
that cares nothing for the yellow flower within the stone   having to go on
to hold back   like a drop of Du Fu's old tears
refusing to let the poem sink into dead indifferent beauty

London, 30 May 2011

政治诗（三首）

THREE POLITICAL POEMS

1
BABY GIRL
To a deliberately drowned baby girl

you're so small you're not worth that chill   water choking
pocket-size lungs   pocket-sized explosions fresh and tender
you're so small you're not worth breaking   only   blinking
bloody streaks diffuse into red flowers   to welcome mother one by one

splashed hands   still in the world   still living
loveliest hands   carved with toothmark bites
when you're half-sunk   your snowdrift is collapsing
pressed under water   a body of water so small it doesn't spasm

directly linked to the womb   your eyes
unopened so they clearly see your final moment   your fate
is a chain of bubbles of denial   the bulge of your wailing sex
all of your organs stamped prohibited

you have to die   for a possibly to be born younger brother
die right away   water quicker than love   strangles this circuit
tiny simpleton stirred up by tinier limbs
and silenced   mother dissolves into a toxic epithet

2
BLOOD AND COAL
> *To Aids-infected sellers of blood and slave labourers in the coal mines*

mixing absolute hardness in a filthy bin
a drop of blood   sticking to your name   drawing out
is falling in   no names distinguished by sticky poison
the tunnel of a needle stinking of raw meat   jabbed in deep

needle filled up   blood or coal   your call
a calcified necrotic lung presses heavy on the breath
and again someone is exchanged for filth bright red or black as coal
some twenty-first century   circulating human sacrifice

you can't crawl out   of blood's mouldy fever cave
when the breastbone's rack is broken   your pit
collapses from burial into forgetting   strata locked
bolted shut on cries for help that exhaust the oxygen

shift to earlier   below the skin the hell of purple silting
synthesises a faked hell   face upon face in the bin
bought once only   needle marks in the arm showing
once   even death has been sold to a lie

3
MEDITATION

To the Falun Gong meditators

inhale   deep as the sea runs   deep as the starry sky
exhale   temperature the pink of a blossoming lotus
circulate and circulate   a human-shaped vessel
silently containing the storm   silently rhyming with the cosmos

inhale   a spot of night below the skin   further than extraterrestial
exhale   always like a horizon newly born
always pushing the music   ears sunk right down hear all
percolating blue   as blue as the pain you bear

inhale another breath of endured life
exhale   two identical blood drops writing a syllabus
to teach you   history has no two sides   the pornography of destruction
puts every human on one side   a wet likeness

sitting   hearing the body's petals fall   meditation unfolding
boundaryless as the heart's lotus embracing its many seeds
the roadless road   even locked-up the spring will be greening
the world   never fear   is a pure poem

开封
KAIFENG / OPEN SEALED

1 KAI / OPEN

kai as in Xiao Kaiyu[15]   and Senzi[16]   leading the mighty Song Dynasty
restoring the monochrome glaze of night
dripping wet they scoop up a Dragon Palace Throne
the Central Plains sunk deeper than drowned lotus roots
in our tipsiness a flock of cranes is silently embodied
(he painted it and you spoke of it)
incense scent steamed a thousand years stays to guard the riverbank
a rolled-up roadmap endlessly counterfeiting   needs no
original   blazing heat on the bridge
like a cross-section of a dynasty   tests the sweat-drenched
tourist   streets as ever boisterously vanish
lead us   to step out of the dust of a painting
vision pierces the lotus blossom
pagoda   top-down restored and restored again
it has found its upward reflection

---

[15] *Translator's note*: Contemporary poet, born 1960 in Sichuan Province, now settled in Germany.
[16] *Translator's note*: Contemporary poet, born 1962 in Heilongjiang Province.

2 FENG / SEALED

with a periscope raised from a poet's home
what can be seen?   a city hides itself
flung to you   the foreign[17] student in short trousers

and dialect   on the wreckage of the Academy   hawkers
no Huang Tingjian[18] in the archives of fireworks
yet there is a poem   passes every day

like a *bon mot*   a delicacy presented by carp
wants you to wait on   wait for a kind of feminine grace
finally emit a sandstorm   seawater

overflows the windowsills   with a barbed look of fishing
on the stairs   you always return at night   inner heart
setting out wineglasses   drunkenness   gentle as salt

---

[17] *Translator's note*: Semu, literally coloured eyes, one of four classifications of non-Mongols used during the Mongol occupation of China (1271–1368), it encompassed Central Asian peoples, Nestorian Christians, Jews, Tibetans, Persians, Turks, among others.

[18] *Translator's note*: (1045–1105), famous calligrapher, painter, poet, and scholar, one of the Four Masters of the Song Dynasty.

3 KAI / OPEN

as in opened to Buddha-mind   why not write a tourist poem remote-sensing
the earth?   like the Iron Pagoda's tip   Our Lady of Compassion
guards the pitch-black ramp like a fishwife
why not learn that gaze? every step climbed
sets out a new geography
vanishing dynasties like drizzling rain   fall soft on our hairline
new-minted and perfect damp   why not smell the paint-perfumed
lake light   lift the coffin chamber curtain   smell the eternal
lamp that illumines its underground self?

the same poem   lies down on the dust of a different time
endlessly floating up from the earth's core
we walk past a faked Huizong[19]   faked Ru ware[20]
faked elegance   yet shattered by an explosive cough
into a sticky truth   this minute pretends a fake
has recollected an original heartbeat a thousand years old
why not write orts of brick and tile that debate ideas?
soar into the air to fly into a line of verse
collage brand new place names like collaging the nothingness
of love   a weary kind of place
with no causes (and no results)
lingers in a landscape no one else can see
so   write a tourist poem as tiny as life

---

[19] *Translator's note*: Emperor Huizong of the Song Dynasty (r.1100–1126), a talented calligrapher, painter, poet and musician, he abdicated when Tartars invaded North China, and died in exile in Manchuria.

[20] *Translator's note*: A famous and rare type of porcelain briefly produced in limited numbers for imperial court use around the year 1100.

4 FENG/SEALED

the Central Plains are a sickness   growing in secret beside the dining table
water's burbling whisper   has never whispered so close
the whirlpool also seems home-grown   newly-served from the kitchen
the great river has risen from your stomach to drown you

the blank background has leaked into incense that bites
drink   in the vastness of the wineglass   experience that won't float away
why would you want to float away?   the Central Plains are also locked in a boat
increasing each day by another inch the beauty of wallowing

the yellow earth is best at bestowing seals and awards   no seal then no award
the brocade zither poem[21] beneath the wheat field gives green blood for AIDS
your fate is to die times without number   after death to grow more
your whisper   whispers the whole world's mother tongue

by waters that run away   the farm restaurant holds on to the waves' gleam
crystalline sparkle of the red lips, oh   undying words of friends
sit inside the poem   with the fragrance of new-burgeoning lotus flowers
the great river's insistence delicately pours into breath

22 January–22 February 2011

---

[21] *Translator's note*: An allusion to an untitled poem by Li Shangyin (c.813–858) one of the masters of the Late Tang style, which begins, 'By pure chance the brocaded zither has fifty strings/each string and bridge recalling the years of my youth'.

靖庐：一首当代古琴曲

TRANQUIL STUDIO: A CONTEMPORARY PIECE FOR GUQIN [22]

For my friend the calligrapher Chen Shemin,
in exchange for his scroll 'Grandmother's Boat'

what's named tranquil is silent   as we hold our breath
hear one word   pluckable   strummable   strokable   pickable

what's called tranquility   woundable   as we sit in a circle
like black ink   Grandmother's Boat speeding by a cup of bitter tea

candle flames flicker and droop in the secret sighs of palace ladies
holding hydrangeas year after year   brush point must be sharpened so fine

to catch incense-offering fingers   strip bare the courtyard in the stamens
Yangzhou always   the place flesh and blood hasn't yet reached

though for thousands of years ago the beacon fires had already come
you leaf through an album   ask each bright moon to inscribe a verse

a musical score   the poet invisible   the song kept behind
spiralling upwards to construct this space

the soft sound of a curse begins from a single string   a string
starts from silk   destroys once   whatever is not aftersound

shaking the deep alley of the eardrum
no walls tonight   heart piled high with words   and growing words

where does a retouch with arched wrist reach?   Tranquil Studio
is silently   put there

black and white like a negative   explosions of stillness swarm into
the clang of strings   yet what have humans ever wept out?

one ink drop hanging perpendicular bores through life and death
the less you can weep   the more the astragals are inlaid with faraway sight

months and years in a coil of incense   burn up other months and years
as we startle awake   beside us the starry sky

---

[22] *Translator's note*: See Note 8 on page 22.

黄山的定格

YELLOW MOUNTAIN FREEZE-FRAME

For Jenny Hall

to see   is to set landscape   in philosophy
both part of the deep blue pupils
stone bench   ridges and peaks   sea of cloud   the infinite exposed
termed a state of mind

drifting over an invisible face
a layer of cloud   climb the brimming ridge
each tiny droplet   contains you
tiny exclamation   as the instant collapses like a precipice

standing beautifully in life   isn't everywhere you look a bottomless abyss?
no freeze-frame is a rear view   uniting
your rear view of a million years in the contours of the rock
what is not this book?   to read once is

to set out once   mountainside is seaside
green pine needles lap at your fingertip   can't be
any closer   first poetry festival in a new home
sailors' crystal jumping for joy   each horizon line written Return

31 August 2017, Berlin

山水铭

SHANSHUI LEGEND[23]

For Xu Longsen

when   did I arrive here?
facing tracklessness
mist unending on water behind me
murderous fragrance of gardenia

when   did living
become war's smouldering ashes forever hung on a wall?
ashes that sift an intoxication lovely as stone
great rivers and mountains like a little essay

let me step up   into the wind's howl
my hearing sits on encircling cliffs
an inky black pine exudes a numinous hand
and delicately supports the lotus flowers

deletion of what can still be smaller   doesn't stop
an ever-moving poem   that never again
looks out of the poem   my love of limits
is near-limitless

beside the window
what birdsong is not the fallen and shattered cry of wild geese?
held in the stone's mouth
scouring a famished fate

it knocks me to the ground
like an excess of moonlight   a skiff berths
at the focal point of the blur of silver waves
the dying poet is always there

heaving a bitter sigh of otherworldly anguish
to sum up the rain-scribed
mountain   farther than the distant hills
who does water   float above?

gardenia-perfumed wrists
are stuck to insane scribbling on vast rivers of white snow
here   death is an inborn talent
the beauty of the last brushstroke caresses all beauty

when   have I hung myself up
to become the eerie dark tombstones around me and
that eagerly-prostrating
art?

30 October 2011

---

[23] *Author's note*: A type of landscape painting featuring mountains (*shan*) and rivers (*shui*).

向东的列车

THE TRAIN EAST

forest   forest   forest
suddenly   here comes Mother Earth

snow forsaken for imagination   Poznan grows from weeds
eastward   is it to you   endlessness of green amber

sealed outside the train window   gravestones
like suddenly-roused   breath-renewed   screams

carve a lotus blossom   whoever looks from afar
is a stamen   quivering in the quest for another

drifting notebook   in a brief encounter with a drifting world
filled with writing autumn   a little church collapses backwards

Mother Earth   eastward   to bared secrets
cornfields on your body embrace Mandelstam

concentration camps decayed in a poem   false teeth   bullet holes
in Katyn uniforms   your tenderly blazing viscera deeper than Warsaw

the fresh savour of ruins   draws a horizon line
sprints once to straighten an endlessly empty platform

toward   a sea's body odour that stinks everywhere when you want to smell
forces itself into your manuscripts   your nightfall

purple of a salt grain dancing on the starting line
purple of dancing on the finish line   a speed of two hundred KPH

never pulled out a crystal   destination
tearing in an amber eye   weeping cries for help would die rather than leave

through the Bible   through Russian   toward you and overtaking you
you   the little stop where all the bad news comes home   Beijing

御花园中元节

IMPERIAL GARDEN HUNGRY GHOST FESTIVAL

1
tonight   the moon can't light up the faces
tonight   candlesticks drip silver along Huaihai Road[24]

like a winding path perfume lures us into drifting in
to a black hallway   behind   the city full of surplus lamplight

tonight   a garden in full bloom consecrates only
the Royal We of a single bud   the Royal We of a single egg

2
petal by petal pried open flesh freshened to the limit like a sacrifice
your calyx brims with perfume
your throat stirs the bed into a vortex
heavy sucked dusk is sucking one Aah
unreleased   that a room exists for only one night is riotously charming
riotous ruin   mouthed stem   imperially coupling
like nothingness   a fluttering crevice fallen deep into summer's scorching

3
ghosts
non-stop escaping non-stop emptying the substance of names
this poem   a ravaged carnival

oh so good to wallow in the fragrance of flowers tight shut
the final Royal We gathers your final honey
don't stop   the sky's not allowed to grow light

---

[24] *Translator's note*: A street in central Shanghai.

高福里中元节

SOUTH GATE HUNGRY GHOST FESTIVAL

1
from Imperial Gardens to South Gate[25]
a hundred metres   across time that never was

womb limitlessly soft   births a double row of sycamores
a high-school bicycle still stopped at a lost junction

from sweltering to sweltering   your
body opens for me again and again

2
each time tonight   in a room of nothingness made flesh
each pitch-black window blocks your rear view
mother   pampers me reclining in the crook of two arms
the wrong way down the corridor fumbling toward these tears
railings at the lane's end   cut away like a heart's stalk
tonight   the sound of footsteps is an echo
I am my own ghost

3
arrivals are all illusion
a poem slyly turns your home into mine
death's local accent intensely muttering

a hundred metres of heart's-content wallowing
no end   not even a beginning
come again   the flower of last farewells refuses the rising sun

---

[25] *Translator's note*: In Shanghai.

和我一起长大的山

THE HILLS THAT GREW UP WITH ME

Feelings on looking out over the Western Hills on a visit to Zhoukoudian [26]

the line of that ridge conceals all my stories
that smear of green   leaking from fissures in stone   sketching
degrees of my age   my multi-layered horizon
stared at by a tiny eyeball of quartz
flat as a leaf-thin flake of fossilised fish
the vanished wild jujube woods overflow footprints of roofing slate
lead the ocean   to a whole-body bobcat-like leap

so many waves of the sea   flood the taste of hazel
those drops of brine   like the earliest ripe cherries
planted in my flesh tectonic shifts that bloom and wither
travelled so far but can't get out of the sound of cicadas
my Western Hills wait here   saturated with my
fluorescence stored in bright day and black night   extension of the ridge line
smashes dreams   every pebble looking for the way home

past Crown Prince Gully   Auntie's homely voice knocks on the gravestone[27]
past Sumac Village   red leaves year after year and walking home by moonlight
brother Lu Jian   drink up   the purple of the hills as I look back on my rustication
submerged in booze   brother Yan Bin   beyond clouds
it was so good to have an adopted mother's care in a bitter earth
poems like bitter boys grew toward the sky in every direction
only they were good poems   sucking my tonight   my forever

the overlapping skyline like it's folded into here
rugged connotations   each step buried in the mountain
this emerald surge that grew up with me
never stopped slapping the long view of the sea

no point in me going home   because I never left
a little fate fixed the first snow to fall on the final end
to bare this elevation no more and no less   flint once struck
heart's pure white one by one remakes all my kin

[26] *Translator's note*: Zhoukudian, south of Beijing, is where fossils of Peking Man were found in 1923–27. It is also where the author lived and worked when he was sent to the countryside in the 1970s.

[27] *Author's note*: The grave of Auntie (the author's nanny) is on the Zhoukoudian road, past the tomb of Crown Prince Yu.

方言写作

DIALECT WRITING[28]

Quarta from the Lius next door calls as she chases him
"Old Secundo"　　flowers are sweet in Lower Boardbridge Path
spoken ripples of riverbank　　lift lotus leaves in vain

he grew up spoiled by Old Secundo
under Quarta's thin blouse   a pair of pips
would just provoke his arms to be held in hers

so many years sitting on the doorsill　　what did
night say　　Lower Boardbridge Path is all his own
Imperial Garden　　every night squeezed in that one night

a round moon makes a circle at the corner of his room too
riverbank fragrance　　leaks into the fragrance of a bowl of lotus congee
no point in mentioning dreams　　the vine trellis sieves all the same dreams

to teach him it's not enough just to pile up letters　　cheating incomers is shameful
Quarta doesn't fancy the poems scattered everywhere on the roads
Old Secundo expects he could　　but dummies all over the world insist he could

write for us　　the book of yellow earth
break and mend letters he learned in a boy's voice
asked all his life　　as we have covered the yellow earth and warmed it

when he can't go home he can't go back
a single weeping roar　　pain that can't be demolished wants just to hear
the homesickness of a little path in a vast sea of people

he never wrote it down at all   Quarta married into a family far away
he was cut down by a backward glance   two thousand years past
and still not wept out

7–24 February 2011

方言写作

DIALECK SCRIEVIN – ANITHER WEY[29]

Quarta frae the McGarnets throu the waa caas as she hunts for him
"Auld Secundo"   flouers is sweet in Laich Brodbriggate
spoken pirlins o haughlan   lift lotus leafs in vain

he grew up spylt bi Auld Secundo
ablow Quarta's cutty serk   a pair o paips
wad just egg his airms on ti be hauden in hers

sae monie years sittin at the doorcheek   whit did
nicht say   Laich Brodbriggate is aa his ain
Royal Gairden   ilka nicht squeezit inti thon yae nicht

a roond muin maks a circle in a cunyie of his room an aa
haughlan reek   sypes inti the reek o a bicker o lotus parritch
niver you heed dreams   the vine trellis seys aa the same dreams

ti learn him it isnae enow ti juist rickle up letters   begowkin incomers is a bleck sin
Quarta isnae taen on wi the poems skailt aagate owre the causey
Auld Secundo ettles he cud   but dummies aa owre the warld threap he cud

scrieve for us   the quair o yallae mools
brak an mend letters he wis learnit in a laddie's voice
speirit aa his life   as we hae smoorit an heatit the yallae mools

when he cannae gaun hame he cannae gaun back
ae single greetin roar   pain at cannae be caad doun wants juist ti hear
the hamesickness o a wee causey in a gowstie sea o fowk

he ne'er wrate it doun at aa   Quarta mairrit inti a faimly fer awa
he wis cuttit doun bi a backart glisk   twae thousan year past
and still no grutten oot

7–24 Februar, 2011

[28] *Translator's note*: This poem is written, not in Modern Standard Chinese – whose spoken form is called 'Mandarin' – but in the rich and sonorous dialect of Beijing, which is near-unintelligible to an outsider. The effect is similar to writing in one of the several dialects of Scots, such as Shetlandic, or Aberdeenshire Doric.

[29] *Translator's note*: For those unfamiliar with the Scots tongue, it is a West Germanic language descended from Old English and Northumbrian, still widely spoken today in Scotland and Northern Ireland. See the *Dictionar o the Scots Leid* at www.dsl.ac.uk for a full description and history. This poem is rendered here in Lothian Scots with a Selkirkshire tinge.

蝴蝶——纳博科夫

BUTTERFLY—NABOKOV

translated by Joshua Weiner with Yang Lian

These smallest   most iridescent Lolitas
Held a needling scream inside their mouths
The air a microscope looking over the deep hidden glimmering tiger's teeth

    You're getting fatter   accent still slow as snowflower
    Holding high   the weird collecting net, the streetlamp
    To make the tryst   in a specimen volume

A microscopic passion is always pouncing on sketches of wings
Always twisted & broken left behind in an emptied room
Next to every poet is a Tamara, dancing   flying

    Like powder brushed off a daydream Uncle
    A butterfly is sometimes more difficult to understand than a catastrophe
    Your   blissful shouting & high style is not so innocent

Turn the page   the bullet heading straight for the father is locked in the air
And hatching   to become the colorful textbook the same snow still falling
The dead in orbiting flutter   around the pistil of youth

    And the eyes in the photos staring on the longest moment
    It's sure not enough to fly to the age of sky
    You must learn to be the pages of a book   to molt the human skin

Then to recognize the exquisite cosmic explosion from a single egg
The past, a daisy that hugs you tightly
Tamara always carries trees   lightly darker   tremulously beating wings

The transmutation you cherish   elegantly laid down in layers
Holding up the world in its mouth   nailed on high by a needle
A tiger roars   indifferent to deaf-mute memory

蝴蝶——柏林

BUTTERFLY—BERLIN

Translated by Joshua Weiner with Yang Lian

The father's grave　　　sinks deeply into many more graves
Covered　　　stone crushing like cloud
A great weight tamping down　　and surprisingly out from under it a thin wing

　　　Leaping to find you　　when you were still comely
　　　Slender　captivated by the swaying flower fanning itself
　　　In the park　　one organ burning another, a kiss

The obstruction of the air must be learned
The wall　　　tightly pressing the colorful painted shoulder
The falling evening color sets off a little shining leap

　　　When your heart suddenly feels this moment
　　　This city holds tightly your ancestral origin, your fated ending
　　　Old age has no words　　　but only the choked back moan

Then to know　　　the thinner betrayal is the more extreme
One kind of force driving the golden yellow eyespot to grow
Pushing open the concrete waves floating above the world only by an inch

　　　The sea butterfly　　　doesn't dream of migrating far from Terror
　　　Flying　　Tamara and the father　　flickering
　　　Carrying bodies lightly pat to sleep the next generation of exiles

The ashes' contents has no horizon
You perch at the address　where upon waking you shrug off the weight of home
The leaves' dark green lampshade moves closer

When you don't fear   to be caught by a thread of fragrance
You yourself are becoming the fragrance   delivering back the letter the dead left
Bearing its stamp of ocean waves: Berlin

蝴蝶──老年

BUTTERFLY—OLD AGE

Translated by Joshua Weiner and Yang Lian

The ocean's scaled wing is also slightly dried
to fan cooler the hotel window frame   you stand by
a foreign land   under the ribs, spreading out, a dry rustling leaf

    A cold blue silk line connected to a distant cocoon
    travelling far   even as it's pulled back
    to another day fully loaded   even as it's emptied

Riding on the butterfly's back like riding a white crane
Under the microscope   the insect's fine hairs polish up
the style of destruction   Behind the ten thousand things is a boat

    rising abruptly   the harbour
    doesn't open to all directions   a chessboard
    that lets you see you are already everywhere located

Waiting   your own smell wafting back in the original smell of smoke
the flesh like pupa   choking again
Tamara   the Absolute of Flight   rises up against the dark pressing down

    Writing   a brightness exacting from all other writings
    muffles the sound of wings outside the window
    crashing against every word   where you sit alone on the cliff

The stars are above and also below
This moment marks your transformation   A wearied golden eye
wearied further from the wind threatening to grind down to dust

        Standing by one   and one thousand horizons
        curling   trembling   struggling to be born in the interior
        the next ocean—a finally returned pure poetry

鸟：来历的研究

BIRD: RESEARCH INTO ORIGINS

the lake drowns in shining freshness   as our boat sails closer to
the sound of bells   feels the traction of bells on the lake bed

pulled tight   reflections of mountains   reflections of men
an inverted bird becomes this poem fourteen hundred years later

still wearing golden ornaments   a golden voice
suffocating in the sky   still nesting in the water

warmly perfumed breast   speeds our boat in
rippling wings carved deeper still

soaring   shaping our recognition
with a lifetime-learned stillness of acceptance

love   this simple gift
leaking birdsong drop by drop   vanished time

honey-sweet words in the time left
the voice of water's mumbled first intent a reflection too

the longer one can linger   the dream will have such clarity
from the hull the lake-bed ghost she frees peach blossoms petal by petal

each one filling you and me   each you and me   more than millennia
each millennium fermented into a soft sigh

slapping forest green   unweeping because resigned this way
drinking poems unwritten   because twice drunk is needless

our boat sails closer in   to the reflections
only a warmly-perfumed   stripped-bare world   left

this poem   asks no more favours of poetry   like love
peaceful rest at the ending   leaving behind a lone bird

a metallic   long ago   faraway message
migrates onto a lakelight-crystalline neck

reflection keeps on writing and loving   we sail toward
sail into   a portion reclaimed by the sound of bells

to find our nest   always new-built
always shining and fresh   sleep underwater   just poetry

舞：和李白裸泳

DANCE: SWIMMING NAKED WITH LI BAI[30]

"My dancing shadow is all over the place"

1
five in the morning   this town belongs to the crows
the sky stands on shining tiptoe   yelling blackness
feathers of water put on for you empty
beauty   dawn dripped wetly from the spring's mouth
last night was all whirlpool

2
little fragment of broken moon in a name
bedraggled white   who isn't that white
booze's loneliness takes me for two   ten
millions of   you that bares your shadow
how ravishing the gesture of leaping into water

3
a thrown Nightgleam Cup[31] turns into the tall goblet of a glass tower
each petal in the bouquet a display case   brow and eye's
charm   no matter how you try can't be shed
booze's bouquet in reflections   dance steps totter unsteadily
a princess's weariness is the passion of non-spacetime

4
plural fingertips explore in plural skin
kneading   to paddle a white cloud
plural fat and tender river   green with floating moons
a silver flower of abalone gets up close to a cheek
soaking sky again left under you

5
the dance strips the dancer bare
crows somewhere caw   your darkness fills
your self   a line of verse spatters some kind of
princess's drunkenness   sprawling aslant from Tang times
loneliness   has no mistaken feet to trample everywhere

6
one glass of booze is cast in the throat's mould
a most private act   exposed to public view
rocks internal organs   blemish is beauty and glory
jump once into the river's fishy stink   then soaking wet
dive a thousand years beneath that fishy stench

7
In this poem shadow is speaking   shadow
wears impermanence   sees moon and light in contraflow
on the water a piece of music and world in contraflow
shadow imagining
destruction equal to existence

8
so the princess's neck has no reality
has a pain that never ebbs   the pain of strangling it broken
so the sky blue of one morning   along with the crows
dancing   rainbow skirt and feather cloak[32] discarded on the banking
a poet will wear that body temperature if he wants to

9
raise a glass   invite drunken and snow-white crystal
invite   love that lightly comes and lightly goes
invite you to be me   but I've been her for a long time
loneliness is plural soaking in each other's sex
lightly   the same glass mounts ten thousand peonies

10
in the sky a great ball of dancing flesh tones
whirl into this drinking spree   contrast with unsundering first love
whirling into poetry   shadow's unwearying desire
a jug of endlessly pouring passion
you   (or I)   can't escape from a painful purity

11
sweet as something inhuman   we can't see
time   only carry it in itself
the princess's desire slowly blues with carrying moments
drunk or sober   taking more and more turns at weightlessness
enough to forget the last beginning

12
crows cascade down nakedness
the town cascades down nakedness
the cry of water   blackens you and brightens you
makes me count golden pubic hairs one by one
another universe has just cleared the dance floor

18 October 2010–21 February 2011

---

[30] *Translator's note*: Li Bai (CE701–762) doyen of Tang poets, was said to have drowned when he was drunk, reaching out from a small boat to grab the reflection of the moon on the water. Some say he died of consumption, or of drink, but no one knows. All we do know is that when he was granted a court appointment in 764, he was reported to have died more than a year before. Yang Lian's poem includes many allusions to Li Bai's poetry.

[31] *Translator's note*: An allusion to the famous lines of Tang dynasty poet Wang Han (fl. c.CE721), "Grape wine in a Nightgleam Cup / I want to drink, but the horseback lute is urging us on". The Nightgleam Cup was carved from jade from Gansu in the far northwest, which was said to glow in the dark.

[32] *Translator's note*: An allusion to the famous poem by Bai Juyi (CE772–846), 'The Ballad of Everlasting Sorrow', which describes the emperor's favourite concubine Yang Guifei performing a dance of this name. Li Bai was an intimate of the emperor, and is said to have drunk with him as Yang danced.

圣安德鲁斯（二首）

ST. ANDREWS

1
holy relics   splattering snow-white on every rock
death's house number at the street's end   commotion
so uncontaminated it can only be seen

downward-slanting   dripping steps of stone
go on dripping   in a downward direction
bared by degrees   the ebb-tide of the heart's ruin

I thread my way through gravestones   shades
crowd in   crawling over a blurred inscription
of the smallest James

stroke by stroke stone paints the bitterness of flesh
rotten beneath green grass   the scene's decoration
is an exquisite imagining of the eye   as a gash

sliding   seagulls study a coffinish
wide open   linguistics of motion
the god we   choked   leaves a jet-black door of stone

and   that faraway indigo slash
is pure and perfectly simple gradation
notched inside the gaze   the other side of emptiness is the ocean

2
in the darkness   your face sketches a phosphorescent contour
first sight of a huge moon for nineteen years
stuck to the train window   this night is the road of return

billows quickening beside your lips
insert you in the tightly inserted glass
and the ocean's mirrored   torn-down purity

to run into a friend is to run into an illness
a kind of beauty   to go home is to go back into the sound of a storm declaiming
a lonely knowledge that's listening to the sea and growing up

vastness   leaks out one beautiful and tender drop
the city destroyed again and only now rebuilt in moonlight
golden pitch-black imagination   mirroring you

face almost near enough to touch
though overtaking an illusion   a world of missed chances
infinitely small   travels alongside an instant infinitely large

every night is the road of return
on the seat beside me sits a miracle
you have turned into a poem   lighting up a caved-in everything

U1，玉台新咏站

U1, STATION *NEW SONGS FROM A JADE TERRACE* [33]

a million glittering screws fixed to go nowhere
the million times sucked moon half-paralysed here
the two-way chanted tunnel   squeezes the same black

a fifteen-hundred-year-old love song   awaits your singing voice
puts down a piece of jade   drunkards make a date at the underworld's door
a false tepidity crammed with broken bottles   leaking out puff by puff

from formed words long weary of celebration   line by line by line again
and other people heaped on a sheet of newspaper   breeze you long for, sir
a stench of death fills the air   east to Warsaw   further east still

in the destroyed bronze mirror   a girl sits pencilling her brows again
is it you?   gold bed-curtain on a steel bench in the station
looks   bloom and wither underground   one pale brown pistil

only get close to your own season   snow filling the city
in distant sight descend if you want   your amber eyes scan
a timetable hidden deeper   a night of boundlessness closing in

boundlessness pushes away   two never-intersecting horizons
buried in your heart   sing   a jade yearning that never ends
for fifteen hundred years tight-wound vagrant gypsy strings

keen blades of love songs   skin and mount a specimen peacock
pain   builds a nest for you   souls crowd underneath the tracks
each point of phosphorescence   when love can't be filled in   lovesick trills

all come returning   to adorn the inhaled perfume of the pistil's name
winter sun's footsteps tap on train windows   bloodshot reflects bloodshot
forces the wounding of a language into poetry

                                        you write
steel's deeply-felt secret   many-splendoured   rumbling by
next stop, then   precipices refreshed by jade   still silent for you

[33] *Author's Note*: U1 is line 1 of the Berlin U-Bahn underground railway.

Translator's note: New Songs from a Jade Terrace is a 6th century anthology of 670 poems in the romantic "palace style", possibly compiled by Xu Ling (CE507–583).

柏拉图学园陶书

WORDS ON A POTSHERD IN THE PLATONIC ACADEMY[34]

like fish-scales the Acropolis melts in the sky
blue drips on down like oil   olive trees hot enough to turn bitter
the logic of the cicadas' song holds leaves and empty gutters in its mouth
makes Athens a deep sea   and we on the seabed
shatter   a potsherd shakes lines that listened to lectures
on a bottle   the dust of two millennia restored
the fishy stench wafting from gills   floods pine needles and sunlight
makes noon impassable   can't go back either
smoothing our parched   kiln-dried lips
not dodging Homer's blindness

history still indulges in imagination   this pair of snuggling bodies
grow perfect painted once   holding the pleats
paring away a shoulder like a girl's   newly
grown wings   snuggling into a thirst folded into the sky
the sound of water ripples out from inside the bottle
we rub every apex   tender wreckage
leaning into every step   oh so hard to walk to here
hear that Athenian accent say   our destruction was full long ago
a poem doomed to exile is doomed to split
the blank stele of caresses   the blank stele of pain

the quivering of flesh completes the writing
flesh   quivering once for two millennia   like a pile of rubble
sitting on the ground   sighing a bottle's torn moan
noon's blazing cage   tags along behind the camera shutters
wandering everywhere   shutting page by page the human-shaped gardens
a potsherd's dark red tongue licks
a sex appeal death lies across   that reposes on the seabed

has buffed our drowning bright   an empty gutter in the shadow of the trees
mumbles to itself   balances clay's shattered and shattered again silence
the shrubby grove all around   unloads shields mottled green with corrosion

[34] *Author's note*: The ruins of the Platonic Academy are directly overlooked by the Acropolis. I went there specially in the summer of 2017, during the Athens International Poetry Festival. Strolling among the rubble and the shrubbery, I imagined all the worthies who had come here 2,500 years ago; my mind was bubbling with ideas, and I was deeply moved. By pure chance I kicked up a terracotta potsherd, and though it had none of the beautiful line drawings found on ancient Greek pots, there was no harm in fancying it to be a fragment of one. That is how poems come into being.

巴茨朵夫的鹤鸣

THE CRY OF CRANES IN BASSDORF[35]
For Cornelie von Bismarck

life has one string
darkness has one string
twisting a tiny throat   go back home

lake water is vacant land
put into hearing so early   a tongue tip
opens the red pine woods   a Song Dynasty fan

cranes waking   notes bivouacked in the score waken
light-years carve with care a
sopping wet dredged-up feather

there are wingtips   the journey begins dangling in the air again
there are eye pupils   the skyline is still a wound
inviting you to fall endlessly into the impulse

cries toward home in voice after voice
home   records the waiting immensity
how often quieted   to be shattered so often

crane necks curve down   dive into   the dull pain of waterweed
upstairs bedroom window covered by dense foliage
ears expect bass green   fate green

elegy is coming back   elegy never goes away
until the shyest bodies
move into and fill our growth rings

[35] *Author's note*: Bassdorf is the name of a little hamlet in Germany where there are only three households. One is the summer retreat of the family of my good friend Cornelie von Bismarck, who is a direct descendant of the composer Mendelssohn's brother, and is now a board-member of the Mendelssohn Society. The Mendelssohn family were Jewish, and were ennobled following the success of the Mendelssohn Bank: the bank's badge is a crane, and Bassdorf is on the cranes' migration route. As guests there one summer, we were regularly woken in the early morning by the crying of the cranes, and we seemed, in the darkness, to have been set inside a painting of a flock of cranes by Song Dynasty Emperor Huizong (1082-1135). Cranes migrate endlessly, always coming home by the same route. Yet, for us, with painful memories of German Jewry, and with our own wandering from place to place, the meaning of 'home' is so complicated, and so serious. I made the poem with this in mind.

蝶之湖

BUTTERFLY LAKE[36]
 Inscription for Yoyo's Berlin Lakes paintings

one butterfly wing covers up the whole lake
another trembles in your heart   brushed-off powder
unfastens a roomful of waves and tree shadows   a clump of reeds
turn golden overnight as a peacock settles punctually on the windowsill

one butterfly wing spreads glittering eyes
another closes   dives into the drift of drifts
oh see   tiny rainbows you stack on the crest of every wave
like railings   counting ungraspable   leaking-away days

painting carries a home   endlessly dives hugging hefty love tight
Berlin is yours   the summer's one and only peacock
comes looking for you   wants you to fly   overtakes lightly-tripping troubles

wants us endlessly reaching one stabbing   sweet instant
leaps into a transformed body swallowed by the sound of water
an artwork sucks the incomplete life dry

---

[36] *Author's note*: In 2012, when we moved from London to Berlin, I was reading Nabokov's memoir, *Speak, Memory*. Nabokov was, famously, a butterfly collector and a lepidopterist: between all the pages of the book flutter gorgeous dancing butterflies, and the loveliest of them all is Nabokov's limpid and exquisite style. Unbelievably, when everything had been moved out and our London home was empty, a matchlessly beautiful butterfly was suddenly fluttering outside the kitchen window, the two enormous staring yellow eyes on its rusty red wings like the coloured circles on a peacock's tail: it perched there for a moment then flew away. I subsequently found that it was a Peacock Butterfly, and that brief encounter set me writing three butterfly poems. As luck would have it, when I went to Hungary in summer 2018 for the Janus Pannonius International Poetry Prize, not only did I read 'Butterfly-Berlin' there, my acceptance speech was also entitled A Sea Butterfly. When I got home to Berlin the next day, strangely, another Peacock Butterfly came out of nowhere, to perch on the kitchen windowsill of our Berlin home. Two visits, six years apart – could it be the same butterfly? Or was it a peacock? That shape-changing, dreaming butterfly – was it Zhuangzi's butterfly, or Zhuangzi himself? This poem, written for the Berlin Lakes series of paintings, can be seen as a welcome to those lovely and mysterious departed souls.

守月

GUARDING THE MOON

the full moon has used up imagery
2011   Sarajevo
gasping silver sheen on my window

reflects a luminous watch   tick tock
ticking   battery charged
taken from a decomposing wrist

war guards two years old
flesh stirred into dark brown mud
counting the time inside death

the second hand points at moonlight –
fat white maggots drop one by one from an eye socket –
a watch mildly running as a sadist

reckons how much stamina is needed after death
endures the softly-brushed
sheen of archaeology

my lover   your nakedness
a full moon night after night   releasing fresh fragrance
but wishing it never to be an image   never to be poetry

我认识一把泥土

I KNOW A HANDFUL OF EARTH

(A painful song of benediction.)

I know a handful of earth   once it was a hand
I know this luminous watch   worn on a vanished wrist
still counting brown   bitter caresses

war writes a love poem   tick-tock tick-tock
blending days of you and me   shared fingers
stab the night   I know the hinge-creaking moon

pulls up a radiance that stifles so many worlds
one watch opens its one glittering eye   sees
flesh I know   will never stop snuggling in

on a Sunday gloomy as a requiem
stone's pallid petals   leaning on a pallid casement
a brown   bitter   moment of caresses

I know a handful of earth   its every sigh
wounding poetry   as it brings poetry
sending back broken love from a hastily-dug heaven

冰川诗·（四首）

FOUR GLACIER POEMS

1   GLACIER POEM: MOONSTONE
            For Julia

the moon is postponed to rise like a poem
must do   the valley too sinks deep in ice's eye
everything you see is ice   carrying the scars in a round
the lovely girl you can't see is torn from her roots
golden dissolving   into an ugly naked rock
filled the cave of the lens with the dripping of water
piece of cold little snow-white cheek stuck to you and crooning
stuck to you and sliding away   lovesickness contingent on the listening ear
who rustling withdraws from the surplus darkness of the cliff's other side?

a poem too   resembles a terrifyingly over-heated body
waiting a while longer is the laziest violence
the full moon arrives as a fragment   to proofread the book of the summit
silver shines like an afterlife that can be a pillow to dream on
unforgettable handwriting reveals unforgettable ruthlessness

2   GLACIER POEM: BLACK TONGUE JOTTINGS
For W.N. Herbert

this poem is a new scratch of a glacier
an ashy mother tongue doesn't let you go
puts its tongue into inky black   languidly drips water
you must fly six thousand miles to add one day of Tibetan antelopes
chasing to hear the crackle of fracturing underfoot

every dark green passage pulls a gruff whisper along
on the left the Old High Light climbs a spiral stair of ice
on the right is earth's core   crevices exquisite as
a Scottish cloud   the guide didn't hear that seagull
yet your upraised cell phone records jet-black confidences leaked
by the lapping-closer tide   from tongue root
to tongue tip   this poem sucks in the chill air of the hometown accent
unhurriedly muzzling the hills aside

on the sea's dilapidated castle   witches have just passed by
in their mouths Macbeth's hands   that will never wash clean

3 GLACIER POEM: DOWNHILL
For an Invisible Travelling Companion

the dark flatiron in mid-air that scalds you is real
between the cliffs the moon hallucination made up in three hours is not real
hearing yourself throw down every stone is real
snow extracts bloodstains   words turned over again and again by feet are not real
this drop of water is the Rhine   Adrian towering above
stag horn bicycles breed to become a downstream zoo
your sex seeping into salty mist everywhere is real
the old chain bridge binding the end of night   can't bear to decay into art
is not real   sounds of falling water push a lover to fall
outstretched right hand propping up the void   imagination deafens you
the enchantment of the water's voice is like the world forsaking you and fleeing
the birthplace is real   being born is not real
twilight torches underfoot light up twelve inches away
leave distance a life time flowing   rub once
wet through is real   look round   the dark of you and you
struck dumb by the ruby of the entire valley in the dawning
even a poem is not real   the only reality
is you still haven't arrived

4. GLACIER POEM: SPIRITUALS
For Omran Sahali, Harvey[37], and Karin[38]

gold-embroidered flowers on deep blue curtains
do they flow downward too? not many
not few   as a lamp wakes
the whole room's bitter silence holding
the dark chrysanthemums of friends   hearing that ice tongue
fully loaded with the melancholy heat of chromosomes

the worst news   gives a skyline of ringing shears
the absence of a human form   a face
just spoken won't cease to be   then language
tears itself to shreds like a sexy but
faithless fatal illness   ice is a guesthouse
makes you all rest a while   wait for the dark

overtake a little finger dripping with
meltwater   death's murmur set to music
scrapes the raggedness of an ice jaw
the departure of all of you has one name in common
ancient Persia like silverware sunk on the riverbed
the lowlands of Scotland deeper and wetter

the Rhine recites with the purest clarity
a smiling nightmare   presses on the graveyard like a cloud
evacuates again over the vacant lot of love   greening asks
is there really an existence or not? water's door
is left unlocked close behind whose back? poetry is brocade-bright heart
fallen out of the fickle destiny of fat

a poet bitterly brews a lifetime   to win back
(Harvey said) a wild and ancient beauty
a rhyme scheme pushed you all toward rebirth
to be a frozen form   a bright inhuman light
compiles the forms of cold rain   one drop
drips only once through a million realities

listen to the hand of illness making the curtain quiver
slow slow decline   the homesickness of words
stripped to its end actually a homesickness for the starry sky
eyes that look upwards in time expecting
a collapse   pouring down like death   cherish
where snow and ice's imagining goes: *immortality*

[37] *Translator's note*: The late Harvey Holton, poet, and the translator's twin brother.
[38] *Translator's note*: The late German poet Karin Hempel-Soos. See note 40 below.

莫斯科：相对的民谣

MOSCOW: AN ALMOST BALLAD[39]

1
Yi Lei's smile won't be coming back
Ivan the Terrible's grey beard still tilts up above the still-unfrozen Moskva River
an empty grand piano plays to an empty twilight
one worn-out snowflake   has worn out the poetess's bronze shoulder
        departed souls waiting   for a day to take me on the road
Yi Lei keeps smiling   her cold active and not passive now
her pain squeezed into the green blanket on the bed in someone else's old home
curling handwriting like footprints   warms with the collapse of a person's shape
here only   sisters with different surnames can share a broken wedding ring
wear broken fingers   stares   first drafts   flee the foreign land of politics
here only   the chilled bitterness of a glass of vodka
can rhyme with the snowflake outside the window that drifts onto the Moskva River
                            every poem catches up with a firing squad
a vaster skyline sets off feet always violently stamping on nothingness
        departed souls waiting   waiting whispers are airing all around
rattan case packed   wooden stairs creak   a poetess
sits at a desk   guards candle-dim lamplight in black eye sockets all over the city
the solitary life is fantasy   as death gushes endlessly in
a minibus with a destination too near   at zero distance crashes into a heart
a revolution like the final curtain-fall of a muffled *oh*
buried in the rubbish of Chinese poetry that fills the streets   one day only
Yi Lei is Marina Margarita   smiling the smile of departed souls
        a worn-out road   has worn out my throat

2
at the bedside is a station platform   departure
this slice of grey separates and joins you and me
lost body temperature lost touch outside the window
a great scarf of mud tightly enwraps Moscow

flesh is melting   as we recall the memory
the faded colour of one previous second
the car has started   freezing fog like deep sea
thrown into the outlines flesh and blood let out

a human black hole   to drill through the snow so white
a hurried walk then hurriedly fall
death hurried once   love banished
falls station by station down the slope of the sky's sheer height

generation after generation crowded on a sleigh
genius and cheat   living and dead
an overcast sky   sums up so many hues
sums them up into poems constant in delay

a line of ripping sounds slowly tears open
far away   toward the inside   silence
lends you to ghosts   lost in
darkness deep as the heart   one

is endless   the future of a countdown
melancholy has never been overtaken
the face of freezing fog coldly withdraws   forces me to guess
its riddle   a shrubbery crashing through this moment

two railway tracks thrown out of life
like silk   binding the final farewell glance
the space chorus of loneliness   surging
in the wound   twice unanchored

flow in the only direction   non-existence
roll up and put away night   buildings   trains
we muffle warmth   cool calm   like the time's
sickness   gradually enter the black water   drowned

[39] *Author's note*: the basis for this poem was the November 2017 Moscow International Poetry Bienniale, when Yi Lei was still alive: in 2018, she passed away unexpectedly after a heart attack. She was famous for her poem 'A Single Woman's Bedroom', and had lived in Moscow for many years, hence my linking her here with the Russian poet Marina Tsvetaeva (1892–1941), and with my favourite modern Russian novel, Bulgakov's *The Master and Margarita*. The balanced two-part structure of the poem is a sigh for old friends who drift apart.

彼得大帝的海鸥

PETER THE GREAT'S SEAGULL

floating   in
the hollow silence your body bequeathed

a boat of bitter cold   masts stretch out a straight line
rising or falling is all the same journey home

a spokeshave opens morning's field of vision
topples the flowing white you mumbled all night

birds newly-hatched   how they kiss an empire goodbye to
kiss this snowflake goodbye

did Peter ever come here?
the sea deck created once daily

oh fly   a signature in the sound of tearing apart
signed the vastness that rocks the fragrance of your sex

one dark green ossified teardrop   clasps sunken ships
unretainable things all as lovely as a harbour

did you ever come here?   feathers soak into the waves
the deepest ocean would hurt most

Peter's crafty hands   still use dead bones
to design a seabed nest   a nest carved from ice

to leave it once is to shatter it once
smash it once   dive back into a million years of snowfall

makes you resemble a word   sent to fly off
implanted in a compass needle   alone steady in the wind

squandering the sunlight of such a dazzling background
poetry has always been   alone to enjoy a last farewell

莱茵河——"蓝天"之诗

RIVER RHINE – A "BLUE SKY" POEM[40]

the darkening water folds a requiem
is smoothed again   pushes open a yell of laughter   "blue sky!"

each morning comes just like this   along
the ascending cemetery path   you take me to pay a return visit

a river   dazzling braille on a dinner table
inlaid and twisting between the iron balcony railings

in the flowing room   green hills live on the walls
kelpies push your last wheelchair

the last reading then begins an endless reading
come   let sickness be pursuing poetry's bright beauty

oh come   outside a city window a cascading downward flight of brocade
your love moves gold sunk deep on the riverbed

restore a passionate daughter   a face
damply caging an icon's nightly-increasing radiance

a hanging door   clouds rewrite a lecture
the politics of death   with colder winds forges words

that ascending cemetery path   continues upwards
your bird's-eye history   never ferried to the other shore

every fresh flower going upstream fully loaded   is gasping
the river   a monument that will never vanish

reflects every vanishing   blue sky paying attention
"blue sky" a crystalline whispering

your name performs every ripple
on the invisible score   soddenly full of reunions

---

[40] *Author's note*: The German poet Karin Hempel-Soos, once Director of the Berlin House of Language and Literature, was a good friend of mine, who sadly passed away after an illness some years ago. She loved the sound of the Chinese word *lantian* (blue sky), and took it as her Chinese name. Bonn lies on the Rhine, and from the hillside cemetery where her grave lies, you can look out over the sparkling waters of the river. I have been there many times, to wander the riverbanks, and cherish the memory of my old friend. I made this poem in memory of her.

Fado——海的归来

FADO – THE SEA'S RETURN[41]

that line from flesh and blood extracted
like a baby sleeping   by a baby's softness
the distance that compels my gaze is delineated

endlessly record a dolphin pelt gleaming
sparkle a solar flare singing   from inside a birth
dark blue   sun-bronzed words   scattering

the song of millennia waits for that homecoming
for millennia   each instant is a precipice
fish bone silver white into flesh irrupting

fine sand unrolls light speed under the water
on a shipwrecked mast a lamp's light
takes nightly bearings   the seabed dies in the heart's deep core

sing   on the surface of the locked-up seas
the loves of skeletons blind the eye   hurt
sparkle the hurt of a hometown sees

sing   a bloodshot porn
an infant's pain not denying
a reef-splashed scorched orphan   birthing

it's shattered   shattered more than a lifetime's growing
my focus followed the tide in names flowing
grew up   a wineglass of the bitter salt ocean

always just borne away   at the sky's ending
open the window blinds   seagulls
fly in your face   a singing voice always just returning

millennia of dazzling brilliance   clouds by the thousand
with this cloud hoop and bind a little face   gilded
to love the sea is to love you   and the fate I swallowed

[41] *Author's note*: Fado, that melancholy, passionate, and contemplative genre of Portuguese song, is said to have developed out of the songs of girls watching for sailors to come home. *Fado* has the same etymological origin as the English fate.

埙：听者的黑暗

OCARINA: DARK OF THE LISTENER[42]

steel cables of branches   bind the feet of leaves
vainly fluttering   a bird counting heartbeats
falls many centuries before falling into this summer
and the light is steel   cast into tiny tunnels that bite you

a kind of wail is slower is working harder
hangs next the ear   the dead so close   that friend
become family   a hearing grown by degrees six thousand years
should be surprised a heart can drop so deep

no holes in a final farewell   yet it blows and sounds every internal organ
leaves locked into scalding   far far away
raise crescent scars   still kissing a flower's underbelly
with first plus last comes the clear hearing of a day of obscurity

life   small as the diameter of a delicate ear
seals up one by one the sound ocean waves switched on and off by the sea
flooding each other   bleeding together meeting and parting
an agonising blood group for every compass bearing

the compass bearing you go on   imagine a wisp of perfume
matured six thousand years into a shape two hands dote on
approach an ocarina   approach the smoothness of that bosom
kiss   a tender pointed world flung into a swansong

it's all extremities on a round wall   crashing into
a round round orbit   returning summer's jade cicada to
your tongue tip   press the tongue tip of each instant
you should be surprised at the beauty of the unbreakable dark

wordless song has deleted the singer
leaving only listening   a glass of wine passes through unmoving
long night   candlelight drip-dripping   binding birds
the long journey to silence that grips its source tight

[42] *Translator's note*: See Note 1 on p. 12.

在特朗斯特罗默墓前

AT TRANSTRÖMER'S GRAVE

the freezing northern sea is also sitting on this stone bench
a silent eye-to-eye   leaving the amber of cold behind
a snowstorm road is also chasing the crackle of a prow
pushing into a layer of ice   I hear the left hand playing
slower   a stroke by stroke written signature like another seashore
sideways in the air   candles and white roses seem just to have
swum out of jet-black seawater   I hear the inscription asking
Tomas   where could the fastidiousness of poetry take us?
the way you knit your brow and closely watch me
as if my eye was filled with marine horizons   there's always one
left behind   keeping up night flights through your plural seas
Tomas   the March mud is softening   the gravestone
like a a sail in a windless sea   where is the silence of Runmarö Island
taking us? Monica read and understood
a pair of sparkling glances deep in the ebb tide
in front of the stone bench   a little stone pier is waving its semaphore
Schubert's sorrows filter out the impurities of a whole century
pouring into sorrows of mist   sorrows of the estuary   snow-white
stretching to the other shore   water moves   we know that under the ice
you are also moving   a new story squeezed into the ballast of stone

12 April 2019

平行的天文学

PARALLEL ASTRONOMY

it's so green   it dyes your neck a faint green too
it grows incessantly every instant like a girl

turns more beautiful   a faint weight that drops from starlight
gently straightened by two small hands   this dot in a universe

like every dot   makes a pretty face always just in flight
sticks you to gazing on the most distant topic

streets   observatories too   the night dark if you want it to be
if a tiny jade pendant wants to shine, it will shine like a tiger's roar

one star   slides around a dome that can be touched
still rotating in a chilly little spiral

our galaxy is restored as a clearly small and delicate you
sitting opposite   sitting in flying-by light speed

twenty light-years   the pain of space-time
stored in a certain corner   perfumes a certain corner

and your T-shirt dances elegantly through the crowd
floats from a jade trajectory

tiny bright green soul   already on the road at birth
growing up   clasped to the bosom of the sky

a poem's interstellar journey   can only gaze after that lesson
eye and brow carved parallel to a jewelled bloodline

our fine exquisiteness   alive times without number
decants the whole universe into this one time

daughter   wearing the lightning flash
I give you love and wandering   I give you endless youth

粼粼十四行

SPARKLE SONNET

    For Linlin

seventeen little seas flood the aquamarine petals
under the big bridge   sparkle   you gaze at that distant gleam
you are that gleam   open brow and eye between waves
flocks of gulls   shredded butterfly wings   raise a crazy dream

the daughter each instant renews the little skipper's shape
floating above sky-blue manuscript   blue baby name
and blood slowly forming   as deep as poetic
floats up from the seabed   layered brightness piercing the womb

this is how love will ripple   golden curves at the mouth's side
hanging full of myth   seventeen-year-old incandescent
unendingly   on the other side of the planet a rising tide

gaze drowned in black night   one very first day
sparkle   like pain newly finding flesh and blood
every tearful poem   you've rewritten them today

London, 19 February 2011

五十五岁的最后星空

THE FINAL STARRY SKY AT FIFTY-FIVE

For Linlin

pitch-black gulls hand the helm to little fingers
dimly   the night sky hangs above the park's masts
another year of life annulled   between wings starlight shimmers
without him   only the distant gaze of a grassy aroma

only awaiting another birth   is your question heard
who is it?   the sea's roses raise a tender finger
sea like the rhyme between a daughter and his blood
so much time and space in one question   how hard to answer

love is echo too   crystal   brimming with the night's bud
the tranquillity of this place lets its dimly-felt light gleam
sparkle is his name too   it has been regained

zero instant   daughter's phosphorescent feathers
leading him to be born   borrowing the beauty of all the world
within himself he feels that a little heartbeat flutters

London, 26 February 2011

周年之雪

ANNIVERSARY SNOW

earlier dark　　formed up behind winter is so similar
but isn't you

more hastily collapsing white　　more like the museum's marble steps
steps you can't come down

two gardens neatly fall into
a shrubbery　　a freezing pink girl's embrace

anniversary　　street lamps register each passing snowflake　　returning snow
fingers flying thick and fast　　stab you　　scald you

on the so graceful place of the conductor
two breaths float in air

each an unfinishable book　　you take on your hand
leaning on the trickle of melt water that oozes from marble　　floods the museum

an earlobe pink with cold trysted with the twilight
waiting everywhere　　a planet carved from the cold

the wind's wailing knows you　　stands still
and floating down too　　tender six-sided signatures

press the girl's secret curved shoulder
you need not walk down　　moon-white stone statues splashes are rising now

the very likeness of your imagined skeleton
tattered a bit by small hands carrying ashes

the small seer commemorated nothing   but swirling upward gave birth again
chilled to the bone like beauty itself

博物馆女孩（十首）

THE GIRL IN THE MUSEUM 1-10

1   IN THE TIME OF CARVED STONE

the sky's hue also raises the young girl's blossoming
behind the rooftop   rippling from aquamarine to dark blue
one more minute   dynasties of stone awaiting too
the loveliest first day when shaken flowers through air are falling

children are all kings   at your side galloping
pink earlobes' wild billows   too exquisite
too unknowing   making you guess at your excellence
seventeen years carved   seventeen years in spindrift hiding

like happening on a poem   this moment's happening
the book of longing carved with the letters of imagination
resting on a whiff of blood   life is astonishing

mystery pours in   mystery writes the girl
in a dark embrace from the stone ocean
a face   a dazzling smile   meet you as they uncurl

2   ONE ARROW FLIES ALONE

you can touch pain   plunge it into generations so tender
bright eyes   the planet obediently goes on soaring
holds a girl's curiosity   still rapt after three millennia
imagine a longbow's string softly purring

stone obediently subsides   foregrounding chiselled
speed   the lions roar   and a girl stands calm
the arrowhead's tiny nick holds a pool of blood
chases   flesh shaken shatters into dream

once only   a wound of time ripped and rent
has united all the days with this torn direction
this sonnet of yours   drenched in girl scent

sparkle   a glance hunts alone a kind of far-travelling
stone records in silence a moment of amazement
the arrow is flying   an astonishment   cleanly sewn   is watching

3 VASE

a mother remembers her daughter's first cry
floating over an ocean   to hand you a vase
slim feminine waist drunk endlessly dry
daughter touches   dreams the king's dream of passion

this is a treasure not found in museums
enchanting enough   as if you watch her fall in love once
love   shadows magically become a gentle earthquake
glass   hugs tight   nails down the storm's round dance

how fragilely it knocks at a vision so delicious
such a small moment   yet how much it dares squander
between the fingers   a lifetime's glide lifts the focus

a living wonder   wonderful because lost then found
deep time steals kisses from the vase's mouth   rainbows spiral up
one poem puts the joy of undried tears down

4 PHIDIAS'S HORSE HEAD

maybe maturity only needs an instant to crystallise
as the horse's libidinous eye reflects the girl
as the horse head struggling free of stone   reflects a horse
as two distant pasts   lock in the jade of a jewel glance

cradle of stone   scatters body-scented grit all around
a silent galloping has whitewashed the field of vision
look   the skull's bright glory laps at a scorched ocean
having died so many times   beauty on aesthetics is graven

exquisite structure of lighting constantly positioned on
the scene   outside the French windows day's curtain falls
switched off   set against how that marble heart is switching on

where is a hand   to embellish this fine crumbling
a foot away   void and vast as jewelled friction
like sea wind   this seabed-drenched brooding

5 GIRL GHOSTING

two lip lines in the corner quietly mislaid
the beautiful women pulled sinuous from stone
the warmth   you created   softly sighed
to make a pair   shadows exchange their youth

waves of the sea flow in the same creases of drapery
leading dainty feet   to step into this reunion
two thousand lost years grow into shy modesty
nod   twins in prosody   with dreams of the same age

this is only an epic poem   faintly deepening
alive   a singing heartbeat the crowd disregards
formed into pine shadow   every sister is sheltering

your touch that comes too late   but also too early
love floods the shore   you know you only choose
reticence   like an island   endure the ocean's beauty

6 THE GREAT MOVING MARBLE SCREEN

you hear   the wind each minute and second withdrawing
still withdrawing after three thousand years   setting off bright colour
like a ray of light catches a girl gazing
three thousand years   rock's silken rustle flying free

stone spindrift   sparingly sticks to stone flesh there
as if in a syllogism a daughter swivels from the waist
you hear   skin flapping   skin flayed and bare
the great blown-away world   one minute

one second   will a beloved distressed image restore
merely a single   tiny and gentle gesture
fixing a huge wave of stone   there's one stare

bloodily washes you in replica   vanishing is passion
yet the curiosity flashes in the depths of her eyes
another you sweetly licks you clean

7   BIRTHDAY

so many birthdays collected in a museum
every piece of stone   of wood   so many
you and I   life or death of a little sail on a night journey
flesh spews out scratches   as she falls a daughter weeps

daughter's plum blossom bud   greedy to see each petal
split   endless the bloody foam-drenched tunnel
constellations peel off three light years in three days
go go   stop stop   every step a scented gaze

drip drip   scatter   inset in the promise of reunion
a fish scale recognises a plum blossom
a fishy stench names the water   silver-bright motion

on the high passes   this poem too struggles equally
dying countless times   tallies with first being born
you came   to blind the world and me   instantly

8 THE DICTIONARY DECODES LIFE

a girl is a needle   and the bee swarm of words
shoulders this black stone   shoulders this sundial
deaf and dumb the fakes that infest the lips
the diction's droning stings tender earlobes

words only invented once   weakness of words
purely still life   inventing all oblivion
shadows run dully aground on a surface of stone
light and lies   have read millennia of isolation

a retired first edition stands here   makes you guess
where she went   endless pain of breathing
where does it stab   love of black coral in black waters

periscoping in another pair of eyes so exquisite
brings some helplessness   an inverted image standing in
beauty   standing silently alone from self   and from civilization

9 BEASTS STANDING AND WALKING

the front is stop   the side go   this animal
takes a girl in its mouth   her eighteen years porphyry-embellished
to reach ripeness it straddles the crimson portal
so don't move   take care as by the huge claws you are crushed

not far away lies an arrow-pierced lioness
her piteous howl   avenges with the eroticism of dying
vital organs like dusk   a temperament inclined to betray
choking back a sob   allows only ingress   no egress

stop in a tender new moon time and again torn down
walk   this instant on the blue-flooded glass dome
a girl gracefully uses her right to turn you down

paired ribs grow bristly feathers   bestride
living magnificence   in the great concourse a vast desert
drags out   you are the horizon line   a masterpiece of elegy

10   GROUP PHOTO

shadows oversee and compel poems   catch a lovely smile
people in nearby seats have sweetened   the coffee smell
also remember the gentle grace of a snowflake fast flying
nestling   implies a pair of wings in armpits quivering

outside the windows   green shade come from overindulged April
sprinkles a small sea of spilt blood   light speed switched on
with its origin   no one can inhabit the sparkle
only then longing delicately sipped will join with it as one

simulate a left side   a brightly beautiful little treasure
face all smiles   overprints the surf's affection
rejuvenates the surf   leaning still closer

parting   links back to each minute skimmed over
shadows burning poems   captivating as this
write then   be a while with her   be a lifetime with her

斯旺西：远眺的身边之蓝

SWANSEA: LONG VIEW OF THE BLUE AT MY SIDE

body lifting　　surely a seagull in view
leaning on empty air　　in its beak the soft thread at your waist
window eroticism in breathing in an ocean
rippling flesh fragrance　　tiny mast—high garret
just leaked out　　a white skirt shaken into the shape of a wing

　　　　Swansea　　long view of the blue at my side
　　　　　mouthing your bud　　the Atlantic rolls like a premature baby

wave after wave　　slapping the bedside like they slap a boat's hull
blue wooden door shutting out the sound of paint-stripper wind
old lightship's rusty speed　　has counted every fish eye in the night sky
a poet lies quiet in the coffin　　while on the beach
an unsmoothable love poem　　still stripping you bare　　binding you tight

　　　　Swansea　　long view of the blue　　including you
　　　　Into one page of a glittering　　genealogy　　nobody can destroy

skin hidden in ancient time is softer when it's rubbed more
ancient spectres　　decorate the vast lament on the seagull's beak
restitution of days belonging only to us　　dripping wet
filling in glaring blank space　　the Atlantic
lies in your arms　　tiny as an ink drop　　locked on the calligraphy of lovers

　　　　swan　　leaning into the tide
　　　　blue　　leaning into the storm's tongue tip　　flood will come if you want

so long that only you are in sight　　sea horizon
the colour of hoarded petals　　a million times bloomed and fallen yet still you

at my side   two bodies pinned in a long view of zero distance
as if a fancy gushes newly out   fancy
in a million years gushing out once only

    stripped to endless dream   Swansea
      our setting sail   at the same time is a limitless blue return

you're right   swan can of course be called seagull
it's a spectral book as it soars   legends leak from every turned page
with a scented pillow   snug against a stretch of water
body lifting to sweep low over the sea
so connects   hollows   to share the sound of billows like beating wings

    pressed tight to the utterly blue   tickled earlobes
    even wept-out salt   completing a poem that makes us born

嵌死的小史诗

DEEPLY EMBEDDED LITTLE EPIC

a delayed mirror   cancelled sky
beyond a deeply embedded window   aquarium-like runway
navigation lights set against reflections of night rain doubly drifting
a kind of soundlessness   keeping pressure up
        oh sucking   you're like a little touched-down ocean
        riding on a tongue tip   secreting a sweet darkness
and dislocated time blurs regardless
overflows   mouth to mouth embedded in the roaring seam
folding a sky line you can't fly to the end of   into creases on a bed sheet
bypasses farewell songs   round a girl-like so exquisite shoulder
one identical farewell cloud contains
        flesh wings of legs   slapping each side of the body
        seeing deeply embedded night from afar away
        slapping strange flowers of passion that need no way out
we use our bodies   to hang up all the world's blood red flights
the most wonderful postponement   postponed into now
the mirror reflects   unreachable damp patches inches away
poured silvery bright alongside us
        sucking you   a tender bud-like fountainhead
        held firm   endlessly unfolds   in all directions
with only this shore   deeply embedded in a bird's imagination
imagining this room chasing a tidal wave
a gentle switch hidden in the seabed
airport   a metronome of love
conducting a lifetime of flying   sprint toward a single spurting
            one single crash of trembling germination   stuck to
        the very tips of tongues   the very tips of fingers
        in your dark   each dot like a poem   grows as it touches

a nest crying for help   thrown anywhere could hatch a universe
we're like light years from each other   each within firing range
deeply aromatic once again yet can't win free of naked reincarnation
                navigation lights slip by   the spectral room now dark now bright
                deeply embedded in vastness   it leads us
                to go all out to seek shelter in that vastness
                from top to tail it's a poem   seeking form
                rippling through a form   it is here   with faintly phosphorescent edge
                a thing perfect as time leaked out again and again

维罗纳的雨声

THE VOICE OF RAIN IN VERONA

each drop of tiny transparent heart shapes
will shatter   fragments that have nothing to do with Juliet
every bit of pink marble   arrow-pierced
a promise that falls dripping to half-mast

tourists are lethargic   so is lunch
a little bit of meat on the tines of a fork symmetrical with
running water underfoot   umbrellas like eyebrow pencils
sweep the clouds   who wouldn't be melancholy in Verona?

who hasn't been washed clean of drunkenness by first love?
reduplicated syllables of rain make paired bodies
stickier still   as rhyme invents a kiss again
a pitter-patter refrain in the square

puts you in front of me   there
it's the balcony   the iron ladder of the sky
preordained panic   fish bones hear you say
oh come   oh turn pale   we are a pear

always new-peeled from shadow
and always giving the tastiest love to shadows
the poem in front of me   loftier than Dante
some skirt dizzily pulling out the drizzling rain

higher than the carved stone eagle's eye
a certain delicacy   a certain pink   toes hardly shown
glass slipper of voices elegant as destruction
tread in flight on one drop and another

the voice of rain is rain's shadow   just one glimpse
this shower must be forever falling   this poem
must seem a debt repaid for a lifetime
as the void in me   longs to be double

then you are left in the midst of love
a bronze breast lets boys wantonly
stroke   a heavenly present tense
charred by the camera shutters

bright beauty used up   but brightly hued still
Dante in the rain fascinated like a high school student
forced by the poppy's tiny viscera
to fall   in love   with knowledge of gentle flaws

flaws guide a poem   upwards
it won't be perfect   impelling you to perfection
rain's voice   teaches me to listen closely to what isn't there
in Verona   has everyone else been totally exploited?

sung   kissed   killed   written
folded into each other on stage
an age of recitation   as actors' lines bandage
wounds   ignore flaws   where is poetry from?

love peels an unendurable unfamiliar
me   stones will breathe in rays of light
you gaze has slid over   moiré clouds
turns bitter in my flesh   I'm now

almost manufactured   got the message
a certain outward flow in a certain concert of music
shattering plainly-arranged fragments of haemoglobin
no way back   facing your rise

芦苇信

REED LETTER[43]

your letter makes me want to lie down   feel the fingertip
poke apart water's thighs   water's lips   water's stem
oh rub it play with it   a purple rush catkin   vertically writing
a clump of green snorkels   suck the lake my flesh spits out

converge under your foot   swaying shadows expel letters
all with contents that can be caressed   the more the water's nakedness is touched
the bigger it gets   lake lies down   to let you see how wet it is
chasing an unbearable point of fragrant flood

waterly and vastly scalding   crumbling once hugged tight once
plummets down the cliff of each ocean wave   summer
makes hand signals to the only loneliness

the only gurgling drowns me and drowns you
seamless green vision raises the seam   utmost renunciation
hears you snap inside   matchlessly bewitching

---

[43] *Author's note*: There are any number of lakes in Berlin, densely fringed with reeds waving dark green, and when they are in seed in autumn, they look purple from a distance. It was those reeds rippling in the breeze that brought this poem about.

组诗

POEM SEQUENCES

你不认识雪的颜色

YOU DON'T KNOW THE COLOUR OF SNOW (200 lines)

In Response to Shang Yang's Painting, 'Water Left Behind'

1. YOU DON'T KNOW (100 lines)

        white damask throws
a newly typeset snowflake in a ghost's eye
prints   mountain wrinkles   river wrinkles

human wrinkles   wind grows fishtails   homes swallow fish bones
water turns you into a cave dweller

higher than roof ridges of the old homes
      more brittle than dry grass on Wu Mountain graveyard
          more hopeless than the Goddess' blank gaze
oh, water as white damask floods over your head

a cup of bitter tea at twilight   a leaden cloud
        extremities stack up here
rock's lungs   cough up a thousand-kilowatt gauge-filling pool of blood
        coughs excavate here
silted up scenery growing bigger every day
     sticking to shoes   here   turn round and once die again

see   which whirlpool's bleary blind eye
doesn't spawn a black bat generating power from curses?

     a great river wears shimmering lights
     burial is once visible
     a great river leaks into an eye socket shifted far away
     shattered bone and pulverised bodies times without number invisible

you come from Carrying Pole Village   bamboo insides grow names
bamboo cellphone number   dialling to the very end
a silence you don't know has filled the sound of the river's great billows
the long long stairs you don't know   at zero distance slap into the muddy waves
              walking contrariwise backwards there is no you weightless to the end
you come from Steel Pipe Village   four rusted seasons
record black snakes rising at Zigui's feet[44]   The King of the South peach blossom[45]
Cuckoo Village   Riverknoll Village   return in a day and return every day
         a little skiff moored on surging billows of dying sobs
              leans aslant on mountain ranges   vertical forsakes mountain ranges
                   the water asks who doesn't know the Drowned Poet?[46]

a drowned world
who is not a Drowned Poet?
                   a great dam towers high above   sluice gates drop
              a Bridge of No Return you can't cross again   turn and what you see
              is concrete   felled fruit trees unloading their never-breeding perfume
              is concrete   swallows weeping in search of their nests   can't cross again
              nor cross   tear out skin of a mountain
                   sunset afterglow and children chew each other black and bitter
concrete   a river drowned in a river
                   moon-curved dead fish drifting by

words that are too strong   to reflect is to vomit up
                        in streaming guts
                        desolate villages deep as outer space
what's slashed is a heart
what's destroyed is the flesh of fathers who pulled on endless tow ropes
what's whirled away by voltage is counterfeit elegy
                   oh look out from the sheer cliff of the Bridge of No Return

         white damask   jagged heights
         gossamer cover   on a river bed always ready to reek more

you come from Nightmare Village   a kilowatt-hour for a kilowatt of humanity
you come from Unquiet Ghost Village   a water level you don't know
rises to the price of destruction   (the Bank of Hell has water-powered ATMs)
life dammed by sluice gates pounces at death's spillways
        water   reincarnates so many times
          then to be blackened into the drop of today
leaving   the filth you don't know   filth roaring inside you
leaving   *Eight Thousand Leagues of Moon and Clouds*   (not in antiquity)
Fish Guts Village   Encountering Sorrow[47] Village   old men's drums await
                                                                Shi Dongshan   Xu Chi[48]
the thump of the fall   white damask pushing down 27th anniversary clouds
sending the Thunder Immortal under escort to Lord of Death Village
                a great river chases electricity that knocks loud weeping down

      burial once is visible
   shattered bone and pulverised bodies times without number invisible

          stand on this line of words and go back to the anniversary
when the water's depth at its extremity rises and rises again
         dredge up seven hills and ask the anniversary to stay
as endless mountain ranges sink below the water of the inmost heart
         falter   split   collapse
endless dripping wet human figures
     not known by you   steeping in internal liquids
         rotting   the inescapable dead end
   an unknown person's anniversary that can only be forever blocked
   write to the end write in this sacrifice
the point of impact that white damask predestined   can only be unbiased
           pounding the vastness below the great dam's headstone

endless mountain ranges are one mountain range   one mountain range
     is one variegated canvas
        spread invisibly out

>   tear down
>   leaving behind only
>   the loneliness of water

4 June 2016

2. THE COLOUR OF SNOW (100 lines)

a drop of water endues an atelier with an endless look of coming snow
even if it's June outside the window   the cicadas' song stabs you
like murder's song   transmits some kind of difference in the air
even if a city buried in its mobile phones
used to the anniversary's blazing heat   has forgotten the blazing heat
endless mountain ranges always just a fine layer of skin away
vastness stands as a riverbank   a ditch of snow
brushstroke after brushstroke digging into an address sticky with minced meat
Beijing or Berlin   snowflakes lift six-sided
shrapnel   drifting space strips itself naked

the painting goes on drifting   a kind of smear
mountains show their original shapes   look back with each step   trek
deep set in the trek   speech empties speech out
terror's shape   printed where no birds fly becomes
the shape of a lifetime   immemorial snowfall of asphalt
hung on fish hooks   ten-thousand-ton silence like a lesson
and the street changed again is the soaked page of a music score
mud or blood   play with an unweepable timbre
how can destruction have a shape?   agonising colourlessness
submerged in an endless   elegy   jammed in the heart

sing   a snowline dragging departed souls crosswise
sing   an empty trench torn from a rag
a waterfall pushes the torrent-swamped window open

thrown to the nails   water counting its senescence rises each minute and second
sing   weariness arriving every instant
no one there   locked-tight organs of rock only fantasize people
here once   rust planted beside doors like clusters of chrysanthemum
a whiff of perfume   stinging the rear view   stinging time
melancholy hoarded wall to wall in an atelier
is an ocean   sipping at the salt in every drop of water

              ocean's soul   so close
it's youth pushing at the door   a look mother can't stop giving
stops below the Swallow Hills[49] or the Yangtze riverbank   is there any difference?
who knows what groans are shaking you into adulthood?
Beijing's summer heat   grows into the shivery voice of Berlin in the cold rain
spins into the same whirlpool downstairs
migrant birds copying homesickness   return as they always have
en egret pecks at this moment   its destiny never to return
is a sharp one   shouldering a waning moon and bombings
it leaks another day's cloud

departed souls   focus their sight with a snowflake
oh floating   vagrancy with no furthest point   how many oceans
compassing a streetlamp that has moved past innumerable windows
surveying the weight pressing down on a snowflake
turning into the furthest point   terminus of departed souls far from home
dying once and for all in the flesh   blood that can paint a picture
when all the sky is whirling snow   the endless vastness of a great river
              converging in the vastness of one heart
oh floating   yet another reincarnation
man   still at the ebb tide   pounding deeper the wound on the seabed

scraped one time on canvas   the seabed adds a bruise
your eyes sinking below the water
do not forsake pain   seven hilltops sigh out the void of sevenfold hometowns
do not forgive disappearance   in a line of verse   graves embrace destiny

thus is cave-dwelling water defined   you in every season of the year
share a seasonless glass of bitter wine   one clink
and the world is drunk   in vain the hometowns parade their dead fish
thus are poems about homecoming defined
you have never left   June's white damask stopped at the Day of the Dead
the cicadas' song defined the aesthetic of stabbing pain

                the day you cast aside the white damask
whirling snowfall   snow   licking at its own death
turning upside down in the air   stagnant   facing away from the light
in an instant the tearful eye of the lens glimpses too much of lovers' longing
                the day you listen with care to the Yangtze
white damask water-woven   no Dragon Boat colours   no Mid-Autumn colours
black's inner side   that turns ghosts' sobbing inside out
                you imagine days on Berlin streets
violin twisted into music's worst wound   a tune
laces history tight   you know the layer on layer of bloodstains well

as you know your mother tongue well   just invented now
by a painting   a ruined mother watching over a ruined home
blotted milk has the colour of smog   penetrates
your sipping   children settle into detonated lungs
an atelier in snow is infinitely big
even if water stands suddenly to say a foul stinking hallo
even if sacrifice has stilled   spindrift and snowflake
kiss the life of ghosts running counter to space-time
one time   created stones motionlessly grope toward the headwaters
times without number   green genealogy is lost in an epic poem
this poem of yours   this poem of *Water Left Behind*
loneliness of water   loneliness of people   the universe
gathers a drop of tiny incongruity   left behind
colours no one can see   colourlessness growing crazily after death
                a snowflake is enough now
to suggest a watery graveyard   whose garden is ripening in nightmare?

crying out   do we know this world?
a smooth white damask   ripples   have we ever come to this world?
after many years   the water will recede
it will be new   will sweep away our nothingness

23 June 2016

---

[44] *Translator's note*: Zigui County in Hubei, the eastern end of the Yangtze River Gorges.

[45] *Translator's note*: King Huai of Chu (r. 328-299 BCE): Qu Yuan was a minister at his court. See note above.

[46] *Translator's note*: Qu Yuan (c.340-278 BCE). Poet, minister whose suicide was the inspiration for the Dragon Boat Festival.

[47] *Translator's note*: The great poem attributed to Qu Yuan. See note 5 above.

[48] *Translator's note*: Shi Dongshan (1902–1955) Shanghai screenwriter and director. His most important film was *Eight Thousand Leagues of Moon and Clouds* (1947). Xu Chi (1914–1996) Poet, essayist, translator. Both committed suicide, Xu Chi by jumping from a high window.

[49] *Translator's note*: Outside Beijing.

挽诗

DIRGE[50]
> *My music is all gravestones* —Shostakovich

1. ELEGY: ADAGIO

but there's not a soul in sight behind the gravestone
yet the viola is hoarse
sustains   is taking back
the weariness of the strings
its whimpers kneeling vanish
one year of age left
earlier than music
later than music
pours its heart out
not for close listening
the violin
slow as possible
overdue as possible
directness of old age
single string   monophonic
one internal organ links to another
sun-dried   death
maintains a one-way link
with you
one year old   piled high
deaf and mute a whole life
pressing down the lowly planet
you sit
tortoiseshell black spectacle frames
collecting
misery
an unremovable century

the more recalled the longer
sigh of regret
explosively
spiralling
slowly
precipitates out from a penpoint of destruction
the theme of survival
survival in
the line's far sight
hands   can't gag
ghosts getting in your face
dead bones chew
cold's cave-in
composition shines insistent
sound caves in on itself
in the thin corners of the mouth
the cello booms
you move closer to a gravestone
you are becoming a gravestone
funeral flavour
slow slow
deletes a generation   every generation
the hearing
on the same side of the gravestone
an elegy not really real
curdled   set
the same discarding
more than music
less than music
sigh of regret
vast and boundless

[50] *Author's note*: The six parts of this poem follow the structure of Shostakovich's 15th string quartet.

2. SERENADE: ADAGIO

scurrying night   scrapes and scratches Berlin
lamplight seen from far away
all leaked away by this poem of us
traffic noise in the dark makes steps stumble   a little park
full moon inlaid on the wall   circling diameter pushed up to the end
poem of scrapes and scratches   poem of passion holding a stony coral
see our bodies' glittering windows leak ocean waves
serenade   each note painfully stabs the endpoint
tiny nights   look back from all points of the compass
the seabed breathes once   three hundred million years between dead bones picked clean
a lifetime's scurrying slower than imagination   our imaginations
slower than stone   history scratched and scraped to powder
the city endlessly performs endlessly changes   circles
a stony coral's cold lyric
not less or more the darkness empties itself out
death   death in life   wind alongside more like this gust of wind
than any one day chiselled-cut holes going woo woo
closer to a craggy snow-white opus
rejected by the ocean   staring at every step into the bomb crater
lamplit skyline   axles carry dawn light or sunset afterglow
little by little we overtake urn-interred glazes
count time moving out of the body
vomit a kind of reversed shape
hands' bitterness   while they soak into the vanishing hum
serenade such a short little long poem

3. INTERMEZZZO: ADAGIO

under rotten teeth that pump
is pumping the violin's treble slurry
look back   yesterday and yesterday linked as one

what grates on the ear is me   a blank cut off by the sound of rain
a toy era shuts the storm out
just like shutting the ulcer in   gouging out
Du Fu's[51] setting sun   fits a toy universe
cheated once again to reach eternal life

4. NOCTURNE: ADAGIO

                          it's all timeless memory
face theme   name theme
gloaming sedimented into the plaintive and poignant we mixed
nocturne isn't music   cities pass away
and are called back by our dead friends each minute and second
their thorns daily wake in bed
timeless pain   soaking into watery blood that washes both hands away
                          it's all rescinded love
as flowers and grass   snuggle up to the sleepless bass green
history wakens ten thousand times in once   listen   youthful siesta
fleshy siesta   destroying tree leaves not worth picking
only stripping seasons   the poem's heartbeats   a window too glaring
                        it's all the bits of bad news copying each other
only then remembered   no other night but in the cement vagina
a planet slides   no other composer
but the huge golden explosion   remembering this same cave-in
each morning boosts the perfumed impetus
falling from the sky into shame in a bird's head   weary Wednesday
falling from the sky into dust decaying in eyeballs   ever-plaintive   ever-poignant
one note grips soft fingers in watery blood
dead friends wipe away the birthmarks of injustice
                        it's all the emptiness of one person

5. FUNERAL MARCH: ADAGIO MOLTO
Mourning Gu Cheng [52]

forward march   poetry wants a return to our sobbing nation
forward march   Berlin's mildew drives out Beijing's footsteps
     mother's opened ears underground will seek
     mother tongue coming from far into a dream   lifts the translation of flesh
     on white paper moonlight brought together and built love's skeleton
     so shallow it can't abide a flywhisk
     stairs paint in the wind's howl   fabricate a fallen generation
     porches and empty mailboxes welcome and bid farewell to bat-faced dusk
     and like a square   cement flagstones a mass of toothmarks
     imagine unreal selves   shed selves   wolf pelts wiped brand new
forward march   in the blind eyes of stone lions   spring colour fetters
forward march   in gloaming   grave paths overtake gradients of electric guitars
     a child's soft head is a reef   ocean waves hidden
     hand poetry an axe   the axe's blade
     bites into remorse   have swallows migrated? never migrated?
     seabed pizzicato death   amplifies ghost residing in the heart
     tiny shoals of fish haul a rainstorm   release a rainstorm
     history's test tube weaves an evil cloud
     spattered bloodstains every day   wailing words too late to write
     nails tottering at all angles   hammer into the death notice mother delivered
forward march   we are the road   a roadless one
forward march   unreal beginning has locked unreal ending

6. EPILOGUE

in unreal final syllables   we are truly
     gone   you can't find a gravestone of your own
     strings   hang from that little green tree of mine
    weep slow as possible   fall too fast into someone else's body
                           mirror-image reflects mirror-image
the waters of your spectacle lenses collect all the fallen leaves

      the dry pond of your mouth   sips at a new chamber piece
                                    (such a fascinating word, 'peel away')
    pluck   death and snowflakes set to a roulette wheel
    strings   have won when they have broken   you turn and look at me
                                        the me of another generation
                fine mist resembling a gun muzzle properly disperses
nothing left   but music's
vastness   vast as the dead's vision
                                        gravestones transparent

    you pass by in a nail hole   thought deleted
        force me to put on flesh   dawn loudspeakers shaken
            by a toothbrush   ruins speak   blueprints speak
bomb craters of footsteps and files
revolve around the shaft vertebra   the dice of every city roll into politics
    notes die away in an instant   only turn and look
time's one and only side
                                  (such a fascinating word, 'forever')
promise never   oh knead it   you weep and wail on the same string
I weep and wail   a pitiless dying day snuggles into gentle
                                gold threads of snake plant
        along music's afterlife growth
my eyes brim with vast tears   hear myself grow into a stony coral
sucked right in   a little long poem
                            limitlessly light   limitlessly heavy and cloudy
    a regretfully sighing skyline   sublimates calcium from fingernail to skull
        holds a miserable planet together
    leaves
        empties out the names as soon as you turn

---

[51] *Translator's note*: Du Fu (712–770) widely seen as China's greatest poet.

[52] *Translator's note*: Gu Cheng (1956–1993) Beijing poet and friend of Yang Lian. In New Zealand in 1993, he killed his wife with an axe and then hung himself.

四桥烟雨楼的飞檐

FLYING CORNICES OF THE FOUR-BRIDGE MISTY RAIN PAVILION[53]

Translated by L. Leigh

1. Theme of Landscape

Is it a bridge or a pavilion?　　　Both have steps of water
Bridge　　　draped with viburnum and osmanthus in four directions
Pavilion　　　pulling the dead prisoner returning　　　tip of whip wet and green

One fine willow branch whisks down history
One tender window　　　the whole lake drifting destination
One cornice　　　is carrying a garden flying

Who is taking a stroll?　　　Water sleeves dust off poems
chanting　　　each bridge holds in mouth its own moon
each ray of moonlight draws out flute-music of a jade lady

Passing through streets of lotus leaves　　　morning markets of birds singing
Thousands of years　　　push a circling dream that never wants to be woken
Who is not being dreamed?　　　Falling into chaotic rocks upon awakening

paddles babble　　　shadow of that back never caught up
Scattered stars in four directions tear a tourist guide limb from limb
Flying cornices　　　wipe clean the bait of flesh and blood

Both sides of the flower window　　　eyes wiped off twice
water　　　a harem　　　carved into one's heart
The hand that slapped the fence　　　that plucked the strings same wallowing

Slanted corners of the pavilion hang down chill
Bridges are also ghosts　　　hiding in a thousand folds of reflection
holding up aesthetics　　　one word exhausted all flower seasons

Along the footsteps of tiles   of the clouds
from the sky stored with endless destruction
who   is tearing off this page again?

2. Theme of Time

Weariness of bamboos
are the climbing footsteps locked in the upper story year after year sentenced
to decorate the spring that became amber long ago

Weariness of human   turning a corner
wooden stairs making crunching noises   a barrel of tar splashed right in the face
thickness of age   and of speed   the long scroll deeply sunk

This moment is infinitely massive   an arm   lakeshore   seashore
also joins the steel you arranged quietly getting rusty
One person   a pen point reincarnated slowly

passed   through   experienced   the darkness of corridor
looks out at a crack while ships come and go   flowers blossom and wilt
What is not haunting in the pool of blood?   Rot

uses this painting to glue   exposed organs
repeats the deaths that you have seen those deaths of yours
Flying cornices take and let go fluttering birds   tar-smelled spreading snow

Also climbing   one crane elegantly dances
sewing through the dead   buried even deeper now into the magnet
Which tearful eyes are not down looking

at one's own distant place   that many universes have coloured
into a little ink   This and next life will all return to here
in an amber water splashing

Always just dripped down   thousands of years
dripping   a star upon ruins of the pavilion
Your art   found a lotus that will never forgive time

3. Theme of Space

Countless little golden flying cornices are seesawing with ripples
breeze from water surface blowing gently beneath
The room is even more emptied

the cage   woven with words   glittering like words
Crystalline water pavilion of a line of poetry sails forward
What are locked out from inside   are still my eyes

looking   at the space as graceful as the sick
continuing an invisible growth   Yangzhou
secretly sucking all of its massacres

Colour of willow   burned down to the bottom of lake like a sound
calling for help   water level plays defeated hills in the distance
My turbulence   misappropriated unimaginatively

even so   still only borrowed scenery
Lean from the fence since ancient times   ink mark still in the form of blood oozing out
Flying cornices extend suckers vigorously   The pavilion   with even more souls

still cannot fill up   a gleam of fake breeze beneath water
A ghost's homeland left only with endless prison terms
sentenced long ago   concentration camp of a body

Imprison brick and wood   old paint outside   reflecting
the galaxy that imprisons even further beyond   Those 'I's
stretch the diameter after death

looking   at a formation made from water   non-existent
ripples glimmering   last words never more than one sentence
Poetry   holding the evil news in its hands chillingly

4. Theme of Solitude

One person   three images
Pavilion's one glance   twists charmingly as Peony Pavilion
When three dreams dream one another   moonlight out of reach

is all the more sensual   A boundless cobblestoned path
conducts swirling tears on mottled bamboo   that touch and spill over footsteps
a desire to pluck the moon from water but drowned

A person is a path   a cloister a thousand years old
Who is passing by   polishing the sound of rain laid with jade
further away than soundless   holding directions fully

History more fictitious than no one   Wings
four flying cornices dive into a fleshy Guqin
expose   organs broken into pieces

Prince   pursue then   that ghost boat lady
must continue to fill up the wine glass for ghost poetry
in drunken eyes what's written completely   is never written completely   only one line

The pavilion already on horizon   washes fragrance overflown from dynasties
seizes a composition dry and cracked at the bottom of eyes
cultivates   even those thoughts unable to terminate

Three images   blow
a whistle in the shape of human   recognize a crashing swallow
Solitude   a forever foreign land

in homeland   scene of darkness humming in the distance
On the edge of bluestone well   sound of father's cough feels profoundly intimate
sound of father's cough incomparably hollow

5. In the Rain: Garden Where Paths Never Cross
(A Farewell Poem)

Rain drops are in the name
                      but fate of name
          is in every little broken heart
                  wet   no longer able to cry
just like green   hung everywhere its beaded curtains
                  glittering refraction
                    glittering opacity
          just like farewell   always earlier than first meeting
        Flying cornices await here
              looking at you handcuffed a thousand times falling down

We fall down   mist and rain
one form ripples within another
                coming down along flying cornices
        In vain a crooked needle stitches broken pieces
          an anchor tossed into flesh   just like the tip of a pick
            chipping   more   even stranger memories
Everybody's path is an infinite
              end   eyes full of autumn waves
        staring at a distance just discerned
          four tracks slide towards four ruined walls

First poem   last written
          fate dangles every word and howls faintly
    you go   lake shore   willow colour   step by step
                            deleted to become now
      Sound of rain leaks out   a garden a body

                       an overlooking Creator
            Words to each other   derived further from words
glittering fences demolished while being built
        You   with your lifetime talent to catch
            a misty rain pavilion with parasites   a misty rain pavilion with fish bones

Original manuscript of water defies revision
        ours in common   an untouchable shape
                        a piece of pink marble
            pushed further to the bottom of sea   just like moulds of love-making
still stripping where nothing left
Everybody's misty rain pavilion
            shrouded in love all alone
            listens to a heart that could turn white after death
            a passing poem flows into wreckage
                                is actually   true

Houses doubled above and beneath water
        This poem is for you   the infinite
            dreaming your infinity   glowing on the flying cornices
            your eyelid in misty rain   your face   lip line
                                a ray of borrowed golden colour
            Farewell   buried into one's own flesh and blood
shape of garden   destroyed once at every corner
                sacrificed once with every name
        Contemplating that you have never left   painful beauty of contemplation
                along the flying cornices   *approaching you ascends*

[53] *Author's note*: 'Flying Cornices of the Four-Bridge Misty Rain Pavilion' is based on a beautiful pavilion in Slender West Lake, Yangzhou. I was trying to discover the layers of the depths in it, to build up a philosophical understanding of the traditional Chinese garden-scape. I wrote this piece partly because I was hoping it would become a kind of 'blueprint' for the special project we designed for the poetry festival in Yangzhou that year. Five or six world class Chinese artists would show their works at Slender West Lake and, together with all the festival poets, create a discussion entitled 'The Creative Dialogue between Contemporary Arts and The Aesthetics of Traditional Chinese Garden'.

超前研究

ADVANCED STUDY[54]   *(For Adonis)*

1, A MOMENT OF LICKING

ivy's red leaves   haemorrhage
licking the smell of imminent snow

lick it   does your tongue exist?
            do our tongues exist?

dead mothers embrace this little window
still in hiding after death
a place addicted to betrayal   smeared with massacres

beneath the vine's claws   does barbed-wire-torn flesh exist?

walking by the lake   death has a sweet and happy taste
walking by deep autumn   iron railings tightly girdle lamplit words
scattered words   smash rifle butts in mothers' faces
in a landscape of ash the gaze still fixes on a railway line
coasting   it   is cast into 33   89   2001

how uncaring must you be to bear a single red leaf
brandishing   the beauty of butchery?

---

[54] *Author's Note*: From the title of the Berlin Wissenschaftskolleg (Institute for Advanced Study)

2, WALK THROUGH: BOOKS OF BRONZE AND GLASS

calligraphy born from a lexicon of bronze   your choice
the British Museum opens a void   ignores us   as we walk by arm in arm
a piece of jade wards off repentance   ignores the cobalt blue of the ocean waves
carved with a sculptor's precision   dazzling as Damascus

dark as Damascus   a six-thousand-year photographic plate
contains trees   amongst the loden green of a poetess   that Adonis
contains chemistry   lies down into a row of grey children
glass cases silently shaken to pieces   by a certain day

every day   extracts unbreathingness
jade wards off both high-rise ears   intent on hearing the blood-streaked skyline
leaching out of cracks in Dachau   Checkpoint Charlie   Jerusalem
candle flame wet and sticky   every mother will shed tears

in silence mothers tick off reflected shadows
forget   imperceptible explosions   in the thermostat control cube
mothers' hair that will never turn white again[55]   goes terrifyingly black
sets off a stone-blind lamp post on a Ramallah street corner[56]

shining day and night on monsters walking arm-in-arm
glorious as a ghazal   the rose you just pinched back
 a whiff of the stench of hell   washing page after page of congealed pain
downward we   marry the haemorrhaging moon

3, POETIC INQUIRY – ANOTHER EMBEDDED VOICE

can't be real   is that beauty's fault?
                      imagine a shirt spread out on the riverbed
    steeping in the black of a Berlin night
                  imagine two eyes water-choked   mother choking on water
who says death isn't a drenched harmony?
      a little window on the riverbed lights up the show
      riverbed   a word that never stops leaping downwards
                    never stops finding leaked-out sobs
  leaves go down and wounds go up
    houses down   enjoyment of imminent snow goes up
tongue tip   is hooked ruin not enough by far?
                            imagine a self plunging down
    drowning in history's black water   plunging like a pebble
        there's no time other than a contraction of the lungs
        there's no grammar other than a shirt that strips life away
say   death's immeasurable side-on human shape
is filling up with sediment again still not enough?
                in self-indulgent poetry there are only newly-arrived words
    touch in here   he does all he can to pursue his own river bed
                                      to become it
    mother's vaporizing white travels in the opposite direction to beauty
spreads the worst of news   no one saw this poem coming so quickly
                    shattering
                        dazzling as
                              our aesthetic?

4, ADVANCED STUDIES

2001 BC   September 11[57]   that snow
still unfallen   ivy withered into barbed wire
still encircling a distant view of the great eye of 1933
space on either side of the stone walls filled with ruins
sky's edge tears a breach open   as each tower burns you collapse twice
then distinctly hear the heart of an East German soldier tightening his belt
"No Tiananmen in my hand!"

     a poem's anniversary   the throng is a dark cast-iron cloud

brewing a crystallised reality   snow
invisible underground   a string of fresh   rotten rosary beads
counting your hand-counted jades to ward off the white inside you
our hands   stretched out   never far from butchery
     another square heaped with dirty shrivelled children
soaks the street-corner oak   little locust tree   olive tree roots
with staring here and there at the bronze medal of the cold moon
with the iron gates a Berlin Wall made of water can't pry open
one teardrop   expels the unrecognizing eye socket
     a poem on fire jumps down   start to finish never plummets into screams

               (on Potsdamer Platz
          youthful dusk   with chemical-smelling liquids
              spray paints a city   covers a city
                  always this one
second person of the BC of black sand crunching underfoot)

walking along unscrapable tongue fur   the solids of time
smash into your solidity   along the skyline
letters created every second   murdered mothers make us
reiterate murder   stated and re-stated along bone-chilling cold
poetry can't but be there   playground laughter wiped sparkling clean
Mandelstam exposed
                         each snow as the first snow

a poem   destroyed is indestructibly alive
a tiny hexagon can't go past   its
tongue snags on the world   its dribbling more than the world
a little window props one side of us up as we walk leaning together
choosing not to shoot as you pull the trigger like a DDR soldier picking a word in a poem
scribbling into an elegy that transcends every death that has ever been
BC at both ends of a verse   suffering   utterly red   pinching
                     one more suck holds the Sunday anniversary
a silvery white recording   stings the all-pervading
heart   spasms once and has won history

a poem waits until the dead come lifelike back

[55] *Author's Note*: From Paul Celan

[56] *Author's Note*: The town of Ramallah is occupied by Israel. Palestinian writer Mourid Barghuti's famous line 'I saw Ramallah' describes the town and his own intense sense of exile.

[57] *Author's Note*: See the long poem by Adonis entitled 'Concerto for 11th / September / 2001 B.C.'

画 ｜ 有桥横亘的哀歌

PAINTING: ELEGY WITH SPANNING BRIDGE[58]

Translated by L. Leigh, revised by Brian Holton

   who is on the bridge who is under the bridge? where
beautiful hands in the water let go the ensign of summer
they are rushing up eyelashes clearly seen
nostrils flaring practising our death in bed
and wombs one by one are twisted into tools of slaughter
to keep the rendezvous of sword and knife rendezvous of aesthetics
explosion dipped in blood's stillness within flesh paints
the split second of sinking in the mire the world waiting for
its own draft like a girl not yet loved
water's end is everywhere forgotten bloodbaths
suturing paired reflections on and under the bridge
a horse turns it head disappearance of a stunned rider

    ⊕

   the paintbrush works up reality it can also
lightly wipe away an elegy maimed limbs steam with pale grey
a piece of lake hung on a wall morning mist slowly curling
walking us into our diluted selves
meticulously carved breasts of the dead come into view
leaning on the screams of a soaked child ducking out of the waves
galloping outlines flash near and far colours frenzied
like human voices our stance turns from golden
to ochre and back briefly blue all of it real
a real shrunk smaller and smaller kill or be killed only in a passing thought

    ⊕

        the only war is the one in memory
a river that drains time away   a bridge softer than

a body   pluck with a string
the sung music   that can never be sung

a painting wrapped in another painting   her waist
delivers erotic eddies that peel open another pair of eyes

still forming after death   gyrating   time after time
dashing over   the only war is remembering this now

     sixty-five kilometres
          sixty kilometres
              closer
explosions shake Baghdad   broken bits of viscera
can't tell you from me   still tearing you and me apart
scalding steel confides language that chills to the bone
gives us a   death refreshed
bright moon   sky deep blue in blazing fires
is not history   shock that flattens ruined buildings
     they have rushed up   pushed close to us
          the science of shooting
   half a metre closer   history is a flayed skin
     hand-grenade of the Hanging Gardens
detonator with plugged-in human form   right outside the window
promises and withering   precise as the pressure of one drop of oil
     the aesthetics of destruction sucking fall and are replaced
Baghdad has no other ancient relic but the skill of doing harm
          moulding a tower of tears
walking   blankly standing in wind that melts steel in an instant
   being   forever impossible
     outlined

⊕

      the bridge has seen too much   heard too much
on and under the bridge   too many people
        too little life and death   no more than once
each shore mourns the same sea
your white room   a focus of dazzling blue
always as far away   spatters another unovertakable sea spray
lying naked in the beating waves of line after line of verse

⊕

     Schlachtensee   Berlin's hottest day
a girl screaming   little waterfowl shrieking
a pair of egret legs surrounded by green ripples
a curve dripping from a body waits to be embraced
ground to bits   jump to rip the book cover apart
on the other side of thin skin   we picnic
our ignorance   noses stinging with pollen
we can't smell the whiff of blood in tranquillity
in the silken rub of the water's wound   a girl cools down
like a newly dissected horse   struggles free   to the right
looks round   horse's eyes enlarge days of indulgence
the choking truth is precisely the diameter of water

⊕

     Baghdad lying beside a pillow of myth
knives and axes   sun-scorched cuneiform
whose hand   timelessly wields it
  a drop of oil is a god
    extruding us   dirtying us   wearing us out
a burst of machine-gun birdsong rams the picture-frame of mourning
     like a string of not at all unfamiliar kisses

      a self-contradictory love wearing camo uniform
liberates greasy blood   death's geometry wears a black hood
intelligence-guided blood   orders   slave girls   to dance with passion
Baghdad   2014 BC
a madness more ancient than myth   (says Adonis)
        one drop of oil smeared on the sand between the dry bones
          dying a death weary of return
    fake leaves find thorny   beautiful
  prototypes   fluttering
fake passion   goes on falling under the bridge from on the bridge
shattered she holds her naked swimming self in her mouth
    land of murder has an endless longing
   on the land of vengeance   humanity shrinks smaller and smaller
vomits   scorches   a bridge of elegy
    fixed on its point of origin: the Amazon point

⊕

    stare at   colourful nebulae refurbished as structures
stare at   someone falling out of a nebula   vibrato
not known how long it will fall   snow falls beyond the picture frame
two eyeballs of piled snow day after day collapse
collateral for our flesh   in exchange for the art of the elegy

Amazon   picking a broken hand from the wall of time
plucking from a page of female sheet music the day when children go to their deaths
love and hate   equally reckless

to paint   an elegy is our true nature
golden men   brothers who turn to hack to death
brown men   jade planted upside down in a swamp
dark blue men   the sea's verbs are dressing wounds
empty horns   yellow smoke
arms hanging on a stone balustrade   rosy cheeks sigh the world's language

splatter everywhere   brown sheen of sweat on horse hindquarters
twitching   white memorial services in a white room
scattered black   sisters climb the poetic ladder of self-abuse
to paint   formless claws near death claw down

Amazon   finally seen between every line of scratches
now   everyone a blueprint
set before the eyes   recognising at last all the places in the elegy

write us down paint us   from here to here
ancient Greece reflects Baghdad   green of water in a Berlin lake
not time and space   it's life and death
not life and death   summer of swimming naked stroke after stroke
holds the image   swallows chirp   little accidents of clouds
a blue parasol hears the sky revolve quiet and miniscule
water's end is everywhere   a water lily toweringly
props up the bridge   spans   our pretty bitterness

day in day out the bridge comes back   like the ghost of a bridge
on the bridge   trekking destruction   dripping wet rhymes
on a bed   all that's visible is the sea in every direction
the caress of images injects   then takes away body temperature
image of childbirth   love or sickness   darkens that stagnant purple
reincarnation   again lets unbearable beauty   tightly grip
the starting point riders vanish into
lay down another thousand years   wreckage still fresh and tender

---

[58] *Author's note*: *The War of the Amazons* is the title of a famous painting by Rubens, and also that of a painting by contemporary Dutch painter Fre Ilgen, which hangs on the wall of my Berlin house. Ilgen takes Rubens as his source, then adds novel ideas and techniques to create a contemporary masterpiece. In Ilgen's hands the theme of War is conveyed through different layers of Greek mythology, the baroque of Rubens, and even the Berlin of midsummer 2014. The bridge which spans the painting is more than a mere battlefield. It is central to all historical tragedy, endlessly transforming the creative path between humanity's current predicament and the classics.

威尼斯哀歌

VENICE ELEGY[59]

A SHORT PREFACE TO *VENICE ELEGY*

Venice is reputed to be "the most beautiful city in the world", but examine its origins and you will find that it was once an immigrant city. More than 1,500 years ago, under pressure from barbarians to the north and east, residents of the Italian mainland fled to an area of lagoons across a stretch of water, relying on the sea to protect them, and gradually developing this first into a place to live, and then into the Venetian Republic, which dominated the Mediterranean for many centuries. In June-July 2017 YoYo and I were invited by the Emily Harvey Foundation to stay in this, "the most beautiful city in the world", and spend every day of our month there wandering among swarms of tourists along the stone bridges near our flat. My mind filled with the tears of clamouring refugees, I thought of Ezra Pound and Joseph Brodsky: totally opposed though their politics had been when they were alive, both had chosen to be buried in Venice, on the Isola di San Michele. Surely there is a deep connection between them, both wishing to keep on gazing at the eternal and unchanging human misery that lies behind the illusion of beauty. And who is not a refugee in this world?

    The poem sequence *Venice Elegy* was completed on the day Liu Xiaobo died: winner of a Nobel Prize, he died as a result of his imprisonment. This is our own, and everyone's, endless Day of Elegy.

14 July 2017

---

[59] *Translator's note*: This poem sequence has been published in a limited edition art book with photographs by Ai Weiwei, and as a small paperback, both trilingual editions, by Edizioni Damocle, Venice.

1. FUGITIVE POEM

this curled-up child crawling to the sea
seeping into the rhythm of the waves   the rhythm of dying
this curled-up child escaping to where there's no escape

a tiny maggot   curved towards
the greying ones in a row in the sound sleep of Syria's chemical night
thrown out of the window by his parents in Baghdad's explosive night

people the same age on both sides for fifteen hundred years
one origin for the expulsion of all the tiny amphibians
the wrecked ruin of the broken waves

and obliged to be born again
sign winter's freezing fog   summer's mosquitoes
a name hastily built in air   accretion of salty stench

Venice   squirming unseen in the flesh
releasing a child curled up to lay the swamp bare at last
don't know if he should climb out of the sea or into it

don't know if his bent head shouts for home or for a strange land
Syria can't wake   Baghdad long ago crushed   sky's borders
all by the sea   fifteen hundred years and nothing stirs

choking on a piece of unformed lung
enacting an explosion hunted into seagull cries
forging more lovers' locks   that can only be locked up in the Bridge of No Return

escape   another bout of tears folded into crystal waves beneath the bridges
the tiny maggot's reflection inverted too
listening to the swallowing sea ripple beyond immediacy

those shining portholes furtively peep out
a child dissolves in silence
the city a polychrome painting full of swaying mirages

2.   ROT POEM

rot   holds the long rows of this great ship of stone
rot   holds your footstep   my footstep

walking the toppled waste where the Admiral gazes down upon the water
marble window frames   door lintels elaborately carved
the oil paint of the sky   soaks the ebb and flow of tides under the bridge's parapet
young girls' eyes sparkle on the decks
never afraid to wave goodbye   poems of setting sail   poems of dreaming

we pass through time   like swallows startled by the bells

walk the inverted rotted underwater forest
a thousand years of tamping
a stinking deep black growth-ring holds the palette of the waves
smearing your portrait   my portrait
a rotted portrait is invisible   yet like roots
it grows day after day   poking at the sea's black and blue wound
from deposits of sludge rise pearls and dead bones
in the sound of coloured glass violins
a row of dead sailors locked into the struggle to keep paddling

in ship's holds flooded with brilliant sunshine
         gold   always pornographic enough
                  to make humans dizzier than yesterday

walk narrow alleys where water can't turn back
hear seabirds cackle like ghosts

                howl like infants
rotting branches gently sway in the green waves
rotting fish embedded in the silver-bright seashells under walls
the water level   climbs timber stakes   climbs stone steps
like a curse locks a rusty wooden door
like a collapse   another balcony dragged into black moonlight
bleached skeletons   pull another balcony's snow-white bones closer
in the pitch black moonlight sway shadows of people   sway reflections in water
illusion is no metaphor
periscoping centuries pursue their own termination

you this instant   I this instant
the little backyard jetty moored where flows a filthy river
tastes unloaded from our flesh   spread out on the breeze
winged lions vacantly stare at the future

3.   GRAVEYARD POEM

tiny wooden gardens float over the red roof tiles
tiny wooden islands   sail toward your island

green trees bow down   shielding
water   a gravestone, dates of birth and death erased

who wouldn't write love poems in Venice?
as attics like capsized keels collide with dreams
as the sky darkens   a torrent of birdsong rises
a book once opened is a nugget of green amber

as in my dreams   I dream your dreams that no-one can return home

to be buried in Venice is like wanting to finish all love poems at once
sitting in a circle on an island they will never leave the end of sobbing

beside the wooden table   Ezra's fissured face adds a deeper silence
Joseph's cough proclaiming halfway is passed to a poetess
one small cloud   not misunderstood   we embrace complaints
life's concentration camp   lamplight too harsh

white crosses of seagulls are scanning, nailed to the top of our heads
a poem fixes its own horizon in close-up
never arriving   arrived long ago

the red roof tile tide swells   the day's tides swell
ropes lowered into open graves   drag in flowers and spindrift
wave on wave of love poems with images newly dripped from wounds
incessantly soak unspoken love   fall in love with this bank-to-bank swimming
green amber blackens each instant
facing your signal flags

4.   SINKING POEM

Ponte di Rialto   a snow-white grandstand
departed souls survey a river of blood   flowing in the setting sun
flowing between dinners   a sacrificed child
is plated up   a page of a Syrian   a Baghdadi menu
opening rose-red fragments on the waves
we survey a river of blood   sigh in pleasure at the dainties before us

how many waists   how many kisses   little by little
polish the stone of the parapet   news of someone else's tragedy
not in the scenery   how many gondolas holding high
the hatchet of their prow   rocking to the rhythm of happiness
cries for help snatched away by the far-off sound of the waves aren't in the photos
ruin and desolation not before our eyes   look

a snow-white grandstand sunk by pressure from the cries of joy
other people's nostalgia isn't ours   certainly

not every home we can't go back to will ferment a poem
Joseph   your dear friend Walcott
saw a miniature Manhattan among the gravestones of Brooklyn
whether or not he also split open this child licking ice cream

to touch the child curled up into a maggot   Ai Weiwei's
metaphor not before our eyes   children that went to sleep in a chemical reaction
bit by tiny bit turn ash-grey   in a row, heads unseen
their unfinished dreams not before our eyes   no need to ask
whose hand   embraces the departed soul like salt
abstraction of death   don't disturb life

parapet stone warm and soft as jade   as flesh
we're squeezed tight on the edge of a lifeboat
huddled together   never-arriving
rescue   rescue by what?
sinking   where is the seabed of the eyes?
Ponte di Rialto   embracing the river of blood under every bridge

bustlingly flows on   flows on indifferent
nothing can be seen from a snow-white grandstand
not even departed souls   destruction blends into destruction
the ends of the skies and the seas are both by the bridge   under the bridge
the inescapable ocean rises   nothing to do with misfortune
only to do with the curse   a tiny justice is enough for a child

5.   REFLECTION: TINTORETTO'S MIRROR[60]

I   Tintoretto
hand you a mirror   a world in reverse

holding the soot and roar of the tiny streets each morning
holding the salty stink the wind sighs from the fish market
windows brimming full of five centuries   a sketch

trains flocks of gulls to be savage beasts of prey
your families slip out in reverse from their gilded frames

a piebald wall is omnipresent
the endless drifting of running water is omnipresent
I'm waiting for all of you to look downward
the reversed images striving to vanish upward

this morning   the dogs' barks are painfully trodden on
angel wingtips   climb the narrow stairs again
flowering branches and undergarments flutter outside stone windows
neighbours' voices hanging at recorded height
let me through   all of you get through   swarms of tourists
all raising cellphones   two selves each side of the screen
fingers invent a flash   ghost photos scatter existences everywhere
converge non-existence   tag along to delete a girl
a kind of glamour dissolved   into thousands of fake cities
walk in the mirror   non-believers walking on water
snapping and being snapped   killing and being killed   there's no real difference

deep shadow is the only living thing
oil   softly gleams like the colour of night
with each brushstroke I peel shadow from beneath your skin

does light come from light years   or is it secreted from the darkness?
where light is too weak to penetrate   darkness conceives it all
picture frames like mirror frames   you bend your heads
to see your own smiles   nod   embedded in the ceiling of the golden hall
once   I signed five hundred years old   fifteen hundred years old
the bells of Venice again as old as all of you are

to ring them is to hold up   the death of a child
escape into the collective   a life with no chance to jump ship
Venice is a deck   that can only drift onward

a located constellation between soft light and shadow
only painted   Syria   Baghdad   London   untold numbers
a shattered horizon in the sound of explosions
borrows a curled-up   frozen outline of a child
bigger than human   as news of tragedy endlessly holds up its next target

as every hand pulls the gallows rope tight
not caring about the word *shame*

this morning   at the address where elegy
is leaking far away   one person soon will die
a bed nailed to an iron window   repeats a slack grin
the voice of nothing   hospital shackled to dry bones
echoes gratitude for being picked clean
scorched lies count down the remaining seconds
an emptier chair   hopelessly enacting a body
a person so fails to be a crown of thorns in search of a skull
a single prison term   lengthens in from ashes to infinity
reserves a thunderstorm   of nightfall   of execution
drags   a world of tears in soaring spate by Ponte di Rialto

next morning
the puddle of blood is dry
I'm open wide   like new   like before
the sarcophagus of water seals up all of you that checked in long ago

[60] *Author's note*: Important work by the Venetian painter Tintoretto (1518–1594) can be seen in the Scuola Grande di San Rocco, whose visitors are provided with mirrors, allowing them to view the painted ceilings: visitors bend over the mirrors they hold, as they view Tintoretto's masterpieces in reverse.

TRANSLATOR'S AFTERWORD

Another collection of poems by Yang Lian, another chance for the poor preterite translator to step into the limelight for his brief moment of attention. I have been doing this sort of thing for a good many years now, and yet I won't, can't, set myself up as an authority on Yang Lian and his poetry. I've known the man for more than twenty-five years now, and the poetry still surprises me, still blindsides me.

I'm not going to tell you what you should see in the work. That's not my job at all. I present you with what I can carry over of Yang's voice (I have elsewhere called it 'ventriloquism'), I do my best to make patterns in English that echo or reflect the patterns in the Chinese, and I do my best to make poems that ring with the resonances – and dissonances, too – of this strange and beautiful poetry. But what you make of it – that's up to you.

There are a few observations to be made about the work, though. In recent years, Yang Lian has made increasing use of rhyme (he has always been meticulous about rhythm and other structural features of his poetry), and as I have observed elsewhere, that makes my job much more difficult – indeed, there are poems in this book which sustain one rhyme over dozens of lines, a thing impossible to bring off in English. There are also a good few poems here where my skill, my ingenuity, or my patience ran out, and my version has had to stay unrhymed.

After launching our first collaboration, *Non-Person Singular*[61] at the London Poetry International in 1994, where we first met (I was then living in Newcastle, and Yang had recently moved from Sydney to Berlin), Yang announced that he was planning to drive to Newcastle the following day to visit an old schoolfriend, so I drove there with him and YoYo. A few days later, he decided we should visit Steve Balogh in the Lake District, and afterwards we went north to visit my twin brother Harvey, then poet in residence for Dumfries and Galloway. Despite a certain reserve at first, and despite Yang's then poor English, by the second bottle the two poets were ignoring the rest of the company, lost in discussion of metrics and other matters of poetic craftsmanship. It was the beginning of a friendship that endured until Harvey's death in 2010. From Harvey Yang learned how he could use rhyme, which he had previously dismissed as archaic and irrelevant to his work, and also how to use alliteration, which he had apparently never considered before, though he recognised it as a feature of classical Chinese verse. At that time Harvey was writing tightly-structured poetry that used the alliterative line of early Middle Scots, as well as metrical devices derived from the bardic verse of Scotland and Ireland. Harvey is mentioned in, and is one of the dedicatees of, *Glacier Poems: Spirituals*. He took Yang on another occasion to Macbeth's castle, which made a profound impression on him, and Macbeth is referenced in Yang's poetry more than once.

Something new in this collection is the appearance of other translators, Over the past few years, Yang has been experimenting with what he calls 'poet-to-poet' translation. As I understand it, the germ of the idea sprang from one of Yang's organised meetings between Chinese poets and poets from other countries, at Huangshan Mountain, one of China's ancient holy hills. He and Dundee poet W.N. Herbert decided to see what would happen if he talked Herbert, who has no Chinese, through one of Yang's poems, giving a word-for-word gloss, as Herbert had been doing when he was working with Somali poets. At any rate, the pair continued collaborating, other poets were brought in and refinements added to the process, and in time a Shearsman anthology came to be published.[62] I am delighted to say that some skilled and eminent practitioners who have collaborated with Yang, Bill Herbert, Pascale Petit, Fiona Sampson and George Szirtes among them, have contributed to this collection.

I was sceptical of this process at first, I have to say. Having watched postgraduate student translators lead each other astray, it seemed too much like the blind leading the blind, for how could Poet A with no English, be sure that Poet B with no Chinese had understood? How without a translator involved, could meaning be transmitted? Yang's answer was that poetry transcends language, that there are depths to poetry that are pre-linguistic, that he had absolute confidence that poets understand each other across language barriers, and he cited his first meeting with Harvey as proof of that.

I was wrong. It works, and no other proof is needed than the quality of some of the English-language poems produced. And isn't the point of the exercise to make good poems, after all? An old hobby-horse of mine is the belief in academia, once near-universal, that knowing everything there is to know about a poet qualifies someone to translate that poet. Well, any exploration of shelf after shelf of yawningly tedious, tin-eared, unreadable academic translations will soon show you the value of that belief. The poetry of China has suffered its own share of lumpy, ill-shaped English versions that show nothing of the elegance of the originals: all the words may be 'correctly' translated according to the dictionaries, but if neither music nor sense are present, then these cannot be thought of as poems. Conversely, if a good poem is created, does it matter that the poet who writes the target language poem knows little or nothing of the culture from which the original sprang? (I suspect there are – or soon will be – PhD theses proliferating around this notion.)

Dear reader, I wish you joy of this collection. If Yang Lian is new to you, I hope it spurs you on to read more of this extraordinary poet. If you have read him before, then you will find familiar themes here: the search for a mature wisdom, the need to readjust the balance between modernism and the classical heritage, the impossibility of giving easy solutions to the problem of evil and suffering in this world. There is also a new sense of his coming to terms with the devastating loss of his mother when he was a teenager, which is when he began writing poetry, as well as intimate and tenderly-voiced declarations of the power of love in its many forms. There is, too, a growing sense of poetry as a weapon in the fight to heal this planet of ours, so wounded by greed, war, exploitation and plunder.

This is large poetry, deep poetry, poetry that concerns itself with the great human themes. This is poetry that can change your life. I commend it to you.

Brian Holton
San Polo, Venice
27 May 2019

Brian Holton has won prizes for his translation of contemporary Chinese poetry into English and classical Chinese poetry into Scots, as well as for his original poetry in Scots. He is also a musician and songwriter. He lives in Melrose in the Scottish Borders.

---

[61] London, Wellsweep Press, 1994.

[62] Yang Lian and Herbert, W.H. (eds) *The Third Shore*, Shearsman Books, 2013.

Lightning Source UK Ltd.
Milton Keynes UK
UKHW052207300719
347116UK00001B/2/P